MODERN HYDERABAD (DECCAN)

MODERN HYDERABAD (DECCAN)

BY

JOHN LAW

GYAN

Published by

GYAN

Gyan Publishing House
5, Ansari Road
Daryaganj, New Delhi-110002
Phone: 011-47034999, 9811692060
E-mail: books@gyanbooks.com

Distribution Network
gyanbooks.com
India, USA, Canada, UK, Australia, France

ISBN: 978-81-212-8025-9 (PB)
First Published, 1914

2nd Impression 2023

Printed at: Gyan Press, Delhi.

MODERN HYDERABAD (DECCAN)
Author: JOHN LAW

MODERN HYDERABAD (DECCAN)

BY

JOHN LAW

AUTHOR OF "GLIMPSES OF HIDDEN INDIA," "THE HOROSCOPE," ETC

CALCUTTA
THACKER, SPINK & CO

1914

PREFACE.

I OFFER my sincere thanks to Syed Mahdi Hossain Bilgrami, Esq., Assistant Secretary, Political Department, Hyderabad, Deccan, for reading the proofs of this book; and to R. I. R. Glancy, Esq., Finance Secretary, and M. A. N. A. Haidari, Esq., Secretary to H. H. the Nizam's Government, Judicial, Police and General Departments, for their kind assistance. I am also indebted to the gentlemen in charge of the Hyderabad State Library, from whom I have received much attention and kindness.

As regards the history of the State, I have given the names and dates found in the Imperial Gazetteer of India, Hyderabad State, Provincial Series 1909, A.D., and for modern affairs I have drawn largely on the new Hyderabad census, published this year, and the special articles in it, which are up-to-date and important.

I would like to thank Lt.-Col. A. F. Pinhey, C.S.I., C.I.E., British Resident at Hyderabad, for the interest he has shewn in this book and the encouragement he has given me. His return to Hyderabad and Secunderabad has been most welcome at the present time.

I append an account, taken from the *Pioneer* of September 28th, 1914, of the magnificent gift of His Highness the Nizam to the Government of India for the war. This took place after my book had gone to press. Ever since 1857 Hyderabad (Deccan) has held a peculiar place in the affections of English people, for we know that "Our Faithful Ally" can always be relied on at a crisis.

"His Highness the Nizam has come forward with an offer of a contribution to the war worthy of the Premier State in India and of the representative of a line of rulers whose relations with the British Government have been of such a unique character. After long deliberation, His Highness says, he has arrived at the conclusion that he would prefer that his contribution should take the shape of supporting the entire expenses of two regiments in which he is specially interested the 1st Hyderabad Imperial Service Lancers and the 20th Deccan Horse (of which he is Colonel) from the day of their departure from Hyderabad for the war to that of their return to cantonments. But in any case His Highness does not wish his contribution to fall below sixty lakhs, the sum offered by the late Nizam to Queen Victoria in the days of the Russian crisis, and he places that sum at the disposal of the Viceroy. His Excellency in acknowledging this magnanimous offer says: " The traditional loyalty of your house and all its rulers to the British Government has always been notorious and has been proved on many an occasion of difficulty and danger and the present demonstration of loyalty to our King-Emperor and of a heart-felt desire to help the Empire is only one more proof, if such were needed, of Your Highness's intense patriotism and devotion. I shall not fail to inform His Majesty the King-Emperor of Your Highness's most patriotic offer, which I gladly accept on behalf of the Government of India and at the same time express my most cordial thanks."

CONTENTS.

CHAPTER I.

HIS HIGHNESS THE NIZAM.

WHEN, after a year in India, I visited the city of Hyderabad (Deccan), I like many English people fell under its spell. The unique scenery, the orientalism, the gorgeous colouring of streets and houses, the palaces of a ruler and of nobles who seemed to belong to mediæval times, the marriage processions with blazonment and fireworks, the secluded ladies of whom such wondrous tales were related, and above all, perhaps, the absolutism of the ruler—these things glamoured my imagination and made me think of the India I had read and thought about in England, the India that no longer exists under the prosaic rule of Englishmen.

Encircled by great rocks and crags, which resemble the fortifications of ancient cities, and are believed by the common people to have been placed in position by giants, the city of Hyderabad, with its suburbs, and the fort of Golconda, gave me enough to think about during the short time that I spent among the ruling community—

those courteous and highly-cultivated Mahomedan gentlemen who seem to take a pleasure in helping the English visitor to form and carry away a pleasant and romantic impression of the capital of His Highness the Nizam's Dominions.

H. H. Mir Mahabub Ali Khan was then living, and I heard that he was a very small man, but one who had "a kingly presence and a regal eye." He wrote poetry, he was a great shikari, he had a kind heart, and he was generous to a fault. In his principal palace, which covered miles of the heart of the city, he had entertained King George and Queen Mary when Their Majesties visited India as Prince and Princess of Wales. He was the son of "Our Faithful Ally"; he had volunteered to take the field in person when a Russian scare had made the Government of India nervous; and, by the offer of a princely gift for the defence of the Frontier, he had brought the Imperial Service troops into existence. He was India's Premier Prince, the first of those ruling chiefs who make Great Britain an Empire.

His Highness the late Nizam I did not see. But H. H. Mir Osman Ali Khan Bahadur, the present ruler of Hyderabad, I saw several times while he was Heir-Apparent ; and I noticed that he was strongly built, and that he had fine eyes—large, dark and smouldering—, and shapely hands.

And I was told that he possessed determination of character and will-power, and that he had a marked aptitude for business, which he showed by digesting the many State documents that, by order of his august father, were placed before him every morning. His upbringing had been somewhat stoical and strenuous, it was said, and not altogether unlike that of King Edward VII, who was then nearing the close of his short reign.

The next time that I saw His Highness the Nizam was at Delhi, where, at the Coronation Durbar, he, as premier prince of India, walked first to the thrones and bowed there to King George, who, at the same time, and in the same way, returned his homage. He wore a plain English morning suit and the yellow Hyderabad turban, and his quiet manner and dignified bearing seemed to make a very favourable impression on the vast assembly.

Later I had a yet pleasanter view of His Highness, and one that I like to retain in my memory. This was shortly after Lord Hardinge's visit to Hyderabad in September 1913, a visit that had been converted into a nightmare by anarchist threats, and characterised by viceregal isolation and aloofness. Every little heap of stones beside the railway line had been guarded by policemen while the viceregal train rushed past, and motor cars had conveyed Their Excellencies from entertainment to entertainment in Hyderabad city and its suburbs, while the lives of the common people had been made wretched by police regulations and restrictions, and the public had offered up a daily and hourly prayer that the Viceroy might go safely and quickly away. Soldiers had guarded the Faluknama Palace, where Their Excellencies had been the guests of H. H. the Nizam, and beds, chairs, cupboards, and sofas there had been searched for bombs by trembling menials. Rumours concerning anonymous letters from anarchists had been afloat, and it had been said that the man who threw the bomb at Lord Hardinge at Delhi was actually in Hyderabad city and threatened to do further mischief.

Well, Lord Hardinge had departed in safety, and it was the greatest day of the

Mohurrum in Hyderabad, the day of the Langar procession. And in case anyone happens to be ignorant of the origin of this ceremony, I will briefly relate that not long after the city of Hyderabad had been built by Muhammad Kuli, at the close of the sixteenth century A.D., a Kutb Shahi prince was riding from the city to Golconda on an elephant, and, after crossing the Purana Pul (old bridge), the elephant became mad, and scattered the royal retinue and carried the prince into the jungle.

When the news reached Golconda, the Queen said that she would give to a Mahomedan recluse a gold chain "as thick as a langar" (a chain used to tether an elephant) if her son returned safely to the Palace. Some hours later, the prince arrived at Golconda on the runaway elephant, and the Queen then ordered the city goldsmiths to make the promised langar, which was afterwards taken by the prince in procession to the retreat of the recluse, and there cut up into many small pieces and distributed among religious mendicants.

Such was the beginning of the Langar ceremony, which is still performed each year in Hyderabad city in memory of the prince's escape and the queen's thank-offering. And although time has robbed it of many a picturesque incident, the procession is still of unique interest, because the whole of the State army takes part in it. His Highness's regular and irregular forces may be seen in this yearly pageant—gorgeous African Cavalry Guards on magnificent horses, smart Household Cavalry, the Golconda Lancers, the Imperial Service troops, and all the rest of the regular army, and also the irregular forces, the descendants of the soldiers who helped the first Nizam, Asaf Jah, to re-conquer and settle the Deccan tableland at the beginning of the eighteenth century A.D., and to carve out and consolidate the country that is now known as "the Nizam's Dominions." Wild and weird some of these irregular soldiers look while they dance and sing in the procession and brandish all sorts of antique weapons. And terrible, indeed, appear the State executioners, who are dressed in red and hold aloft their hideous emblems of office.

The procession, which takes several hours to pass a given point, is swelled by nobles with their retainers; but in modern Hyderabad it would appear that the greater number of noblemen prefer to assemble at H. E. the Minister's city palace, and to watch the Langar ceremony there in shade and comfort. Thence the procession passes through the crowded streets to the city palace of the Nizam; and after having been inspected by His Highness, the troops disperse and return to barracks.

At all times Hyderabad city presents kaleidoscopic views of peculiar interest; but on Langar Day it seems to surpass itself, for then the streets are filled with men in holiday clothes, among whom pace gorgeously-caparisoned elephants, while carriages dash past, driven by syces in rainbow-coloured liveries, and carrying little children dressed in the most brilliant and varied garments. Behind the chicks of the windows, unseen but felt, are the secluded ladies, for whom, no doubt, the Langar is a great annual event, and every roof and every doorstep is covered with sightseers, who seem to vie one with another as regards the brilliancy of their attire.

The vast crowds in the streets are kept moving by vigilant policemen, but swarm at every corner and climb to each point of vantage, and the city resembles during the

Langar Ceremony, nothing so much as a huge, humming, buzzing beehive only, to make the simile correct, the bees should be of every colour and not mere brown and black insects.

Now on Langar Day, October 1913, into these swarms of his loyal subjects, drove H. H. the Nizam, quite unexpectedly and heralded only by whizzing whirring rockets.

"His Highness!" "His Highness!" shouted galloping policemen, and the people in the streets hastily divided and piled themselves up on either side of the road. Silence seemed to fall on the masses, and only the voices of those in command were heard while a carriage drove past, a carriage driven by an English coachman in yellow satin, who wanted only a powdered full-bottomed wig to make him look perfect.

In the carriage sat H. H. the Nizam, quietly dressed, as usual, in a dark English suit and the yellow Hyderabad turban, and on either side of him were the two eldest princes, while behind him stood a tiny princess, who bowed incessantly to her father's delighted subjects.

Now it had seemed to me that the face of H. H. the Nizam had worn a somewhat bored and uninterested expression at functions of various sorts at which English people had been present; and I was glad to see that here, among his own people, he looked quite happy and pleasant. With hand raised to forehead, he glanced keenly from roof to pavement, and the low murmurs that rose from his salaaming subjects seemed to fill his mind and swell his heart.

So the carriage drove slowly through the silent, swarming people, with His Highness salaaming, the little princes wondering, and the tiny princess bowing, and then returned to the city palace.

CHAPTER II.

Ancient History, and the Ruins.

Hindu Period.—The ancient history of Hyderabad is written eloquently in its ruins, and probably no area of similar size in India contains so many interesting records of the past as H. H. the Nizam's Dominions.

During a somewhat lengthy visit to the State in 1913, I gained a vivid idea of the Hindu races who lived and flourished in the Deccan tableland before the first Mahomedan invasion in 1294 A.D.; for I visited the chief places of historical interest.

I began with the rock monasteries and temples at Ellora and Ajanta, which speak of the time when king Asoka's rule stretched as far as the Upper Godavari, the sacred river that runs through the State, and in which (so legend tells us) Rama and Sita performed their morning ablutions and greeted with religious rites the rising sun. Here, rendered secure by the edicts of the great Buddhist king, followers of Lord Buddha sought Nirvâna two hundred years before the Christian era; and on the walls of the rock monasteries and temples we can trace to-day (so some authorities assert) the history of Buddhism in India, and can watch, too, Brahmanism slowly re-asserting itself and finally triumphing in the great rock temple called Kailas.

"All commentary," says M. Baudrillart, "grows pale before the magnificent ruins of the temples of Elura, which, more than any other ruins, confuse the imagination. . . . The development of the plastic art and of public religious luxury amongst the Hindus receives the most striking attestation in the magnificence of these temples, in the infinite diversity of their details, and the minute variety of the carvings."

Of the Andra kings, who ruled in the Deccan from about 220 B.C. to 550 A.D., I discovered no records; but of the Chalukya kings (550—1185 A.D.) I found a fascinating record in the "thousand-pillared temple" at Hanamkonda. And I marvelled much that the star-shaped *mandapa* there, which marks the Chalukyan style of architecture, is so little appreciated by the people who live in one of the most up-to-date towns in H. H. the Nizam's Dominions. I was told that Sir George Casson Walker caused the wall to be built that now surrounds the ruin ; but to-day the interior of the temple is littered with rubbish and the walls are disfigured by scribblers.

An inscription, in ancient Telegu, is at the principal entrance, and this relates that the temple was built in 1162 A.D., during the reign of Sri Rudra Deva, and says of him :—" He was a terror to his enemies, whom he persecuted relentlessly. To the learned pundits and those who merited his admiration he was extremely merciful. He used to keep his wife always happy. He was celebrated as the most handsome man of his time. He had no equal in his skill of horsemanship, and his strength of body and muscle was so great that a seeming touch of his hand to an opponent rendered the latter powerless."

At Daulatabad I saw records of the Yadava kings, who came into power at the close of the 12th century A.D. ; and who built the fort of Daulatabad, before which tourists from all parts of the world pause to-day, while on their way to the Ellora caves, and sometimes ask :—" What has become of the warlike Hindus who built this impregnable fortress ? "

The fort of Daulatabad played a great part in the first conquest of the Deccan by the Mahomedans, who, after taking and re-taking this stronghold of the Hindus, went further south and besieged and took the great Hindu forts at Warangal, Raichur, and Gulbarga.

I found the fort of Warangal a wonderfully well-preserved and picturesque ruin.

Leaving the little railway station, I climbed the moss-covered rampart opposite; and then I had a fine view of the hills that rise abruptly from the plain and look like outposts. The second wall of the fort I found to be in an almost perfect state of preservation, although it dates from the middle of the 13th century A.D. Huge stones, placed one above another, form the Hindu portion of the wall, the Mahomedan additions being composed of much smaller stones, and apparently replacing the portions of the wall destroyed by the invaders.

Warangal is now a small hamlet and peasants live within the walls of the fort; but still the ruins of a Hindu temple, of stone bulls and pillars, may be seen, and on these things are written, in ancient Sanskrit, the history of the fort and the records of its great strength and vastness.

At Raichur I saw the fort built in 1294 by the Hindu minister of a Hindu raja, and I was told that a huge stone, 42 ft. by 3 ft., which forms a portion of the inner wall, and on which the date of the building is written, was placed in position by a woman. Here, as at the fort of Warangal, huge stones were laid one above another, and no cement was used; and looking at the walls, I said to myself, "These Hindu builders must have been giants!"

Of the fort at Gulbarga nothing remains to-day but a fragment of the ancient citadel; but the enormous strength of this ruin impresses the visitor, as do also the ruined forts at Mudgal, Naldrug, and other places.

And while travelling over the State, the *garhis*, or walled villages, cannot fail to arrest attention, speaking as they do of the unsettled condition of Hyderabad until about one hundred years ago.

The Muhamadan Invasion.—Returning to Daulatabad I was greatly interested in the history of Mahammad bin Tughlak, the sultan of Delhi, who tried to move his capital there in 1339 A.D. I read that the people of Delhi suffered terrible hardships on the way to Deogiri (the ancient name for Daulatabad), that many died on the way there, and that those who arrived safely "pined among the idolaters." The sultan found his coffers empty, and caused the gold and silver coinage to be replaced by copper, saying that his brass was equal to the precious metals of other men; but business came to a stand-still and he was obliged to withdraw his coinage edict. And, later, cholera attacked his subjects, and he himself nearly died of it, and then, being somewhat chastened and subdued, he gave permission to his subjects to return to Delhi, and a handful of despairing men, women, and children went home.

The Bahmani Kings (1347-1527 A.D.).—The various Mahomedan Governors of the Deccan asserted their independence after the sultan of Delhi had gone away, and the first to assume the title of King were the Bahmani rulers, who established their capital at Gulbarga.

I visited the tombs of these kings there—small square stone buildings, with a bulbous roof, and containing a grave of the simplest character. Standing at some distance from the city, the tombs are cool and quiet ; and I was told that during the reign of H. H. the late Nizam, a local official appropriated two of them to his private use—one for a living place and the other as an office—a piece of vandalism that called down upon him the wrath of His Highness's government, when it was discovered.

After a time, the Bahmani kings moved their capital to Bidar, and there more of the tombs of these kings may be seen, also the remains of a great college built by a Bahmani minister.

The Barid Shahi Kings (1538-1609 A.D.).—At Bidar I saw the tombs of the Barid Shahi kings, who succeeded the Bahmani rulers. And here I would like to mention that Bidar, which is historically the most interesting city in the State, is very difficult to get at, unless one has a motor car, for there is no railway communication between Bidar and the capital, and the usual mode of performing the sixty miles journey between Bidar and Hyderabad city is by bullock cart.

Originally a Hindu stronghold, Bidar was besieged and taken by Mahammad bin Tughlak, the sultan of Delhi, in 1321 A.D. In 1430 A.D. it was annexed by the Bahmani kings, who moved their capital there from Gulbarga, and later on it became the capital of the Barid Shahi kings. In 1656 A.D. Aurangzeb besieged and took both the fort and the city, and, finally, at the beginning of the eighteenth century, Bidar passed quietly into the hands of Asaf Jah, the first Nizam.

The Kutb Shahi Kings (1512-1687 A.D.).—After the Barid Shahi dynasty, came the famous Kutb Shahi kings, who made their capital at Golconda.

As every one knows, the Golconda fortress lies five miles west of Hyderabad city, and the tombs of the Kutb Shahi kings are just outside it. Muhammad Kuli, the fifth Kutb Shahi king, founded the present capital of Hyderabad in 1589 A.D., and most of the old buildings in the city were erected by him, such as the Char Minar, the Char Kaman, the Ashur Khana (the city wall), and the Purana Pul (old bridge), which connects the city with the road to Golconda.

In 1687 the Golconda fortress was taken by Aurangzeb, after a siege of eight months, and the last king of Golconda, Abul Hasan, was made a prisoner and confined in the fort of Daulatabad, where he died in 1704 A.D.

The Emperor Aurangzeb.—At Roaza I saw the tombs of Abul Hasan, the last king of Golconda, Asaf Jah, the first Nizam, and Aurangzeb, the conqueror of Hyderabad, Golconda, Daulatabad, Bidar, Raichur, and the other strongholds in the Deccan that had refused to acknowledge the supremacy of Delhi. And before I briefly describe the tomb of that great conqueror and iconoclast, I would like to point out that at Roaza may be seen most, if not all, of the Indian styles of architecture — the Pathan style, characterised by horse-shoe shaped dome and pointed arches, the later Moghul style, with bulbous dome, slender minarets, and scolloped arches, the Jain, the Dravidian, the Indo-Aryan and the Chalukyan—all these styles may be seen at Roaza or near by. And at Ellora is one of India's greatest architectural triumphs, the Kailas rock-cut temple, built by Krishna, the Rashtrakuta king of Malkhed, in the eighth century A.D.

Midway between the north and south gates of Roaza is a domed porch that leads into a large quadrangle, with a mosque on the west side; and passing through a small gateway the visitor comes to a courtyard where a white cloth covers the simple grave of the great emperor Aurangzeb. He died on the 4th of March, 1707, in the eighty-ninth year of his age and the fifty-fourth year of his reign; and his last words to his sons were:—"I am going. No man has seen the departure of his own soul, but I see that mine is departing. Farewell! Farewell! Farewell!"

CHAPTER III.

THE NIZAMS AND THEIR MINISTERS.

AFTER leaving the ruins that make H. H. the Nizam's Dominions so interesting, the history of Hyderabad is not easy to follow.

In the public libraries in British India I could discover nothing about Hyderabad further than the condensed summaries contained in such books as the Imperial Gazetteer of India and the Encyclopædia Britannica; and only in the Hyderabad State Library was I able to find particulars concerning the Nizams and their Ministers.*

Moreover, some of the most important books on these subjects are becoming rare, even in Hyderabad itself, such as, for instance, " Hyderabad (Deccan) under Sir Salar Jung " by Moulvi Cheragh Ali, and the biography of Sir Salar Jung I, which was written shortly after his death by Nawab Imud-ul-Mulk Bahadur. The " Historical

* As the ancient history of the Hyderabad State is somewhat contradictory and confusing, I have given the names and dates found in the Imperial Gazette of India, Hyderabad State, Provincial Series, 1909, A.D

and Descriptive Sketch of the Nizam's Dominions," compiled by Syed Hussain Bilgrami, B.A.; and C. Willmott, C.S., is out of print; and this book, which is, no doubt, the best history (in English) of Hyderabad, and which is, I believe, used as the text-book on Hyderabad for Civil Service examinations in England, ends with the death of H. H. Afzul-ud-Daula in 1869.

And it is a fact that there is no history of the long reign of H. H. Mir Mahabub Ali Khan—1869-1911—whatsoever at the present time, and that for information concerning all that has taken place during the last fifty years in Hyderabad State affairs we must go to the Administration Reports that have been published from time to time by His Highness's ministers. Consequently we read of the great reforms and improvements introduced by Sir Salar Jung I, and we find these things full-grown in the reign of the present Nizam, and so much altered and improved that Sir Salar Jung himself would scarcely know them now. And I need scarcely point out that Government Administration Reports are difficult to obtain, and that until about twelve years ago these official documents were published in Urdu.

As to this little book, I have had neither time nor opportunity to fill in the gap between the reigns of H. H. Nizam Afzul-ud-Daula and H. H. Nizam Mir Osman Ali Khan Bahadur. I have drawn on recent administration reports for information concerning the State as it is to-day ; but I have not attempted to supply one of the greatest wants of the State, namely, a history of the reign of H. H. Mir Mahabub Ali Khan.

Asaf Jah, the first Nizam, was born in 1671 A.D., at Delhi, where he, at an early age, attracted the favourable notice of the emperor Aurangzeb. His original name was Kamar-ud-din, and the title of Asaf Jah was conferred upon him by the emperor Muhammud Shah when he obtained the keys of the fortress of Golconda. He was at that time engaged in re-conquering the possessions of the Delhi emperor in southern India, and about the year 1730 A.D. he was confirmed in his appointment as Viceroy of the Deccan by the emperor Muhammud Shah, who not only sent him the title of Asaf Jah, but also some jewels and an elephant, and told him "to settle the country, repress the turbulent, punish the rebels, and cherish the people." He went several times to the assistance of the emperor at Delhi, and "all his undertakings shed a new lustre on the house of Timur," and "he never moved a hair's breadth in opposition to the Imperial dynasty." In 1742 he formed projects for conquering the Carnatic, and in 1748 he died in camp, near Burhanpur, and his body was interred near the fort of Daulatabad, where his tomb may be seen to-day.

He was succeeded by his second son, Nasir Jung, who had rebelled against him in 1740 A.D., and had then been made a prisoner and confined in the fortress of Kandahar, near Nander. During the reign of this Nizam, M. Dupleix, the governor of the French possessions in India, began to intrigue in Hyderabad, and Nasir Jung collected a large army and marched on Pondicherry. But he was killed by one of his own followers before he could accomplish his project, and in 1750 A.D. he was succeeded by Muzaffar Jung, M. Dupleix's puppet.

A very interesting account of Muzaffar Jung's visit to Pondicherry and his installation there by M. Dupleix as Subedar of the Carnatic may be found in the French Library at Pondicherry; and we learn that he tried to arrange a marriage between the emperor of Delhi and Mlle. Chou-Chou, the step-daughter of M. Dupleix, and that that astute Frenchman had some difficulty in refusing the honour that the Delhi emperor desired to confer upon his family.

Muzaffar Jung was murdered during his return journey, and M. Bussy, the commander of the French troops that had accompanied him, then persuaded the people of Hyderabad to place Salabat Jung upon the *gadi*. This was done in 1751, and afterwards the French gained much influence in Hyderabad, where territory was assigned to them for the support of their troops. But in 1755, when hostilities commenced in Europe between the French and the English, M. Bussy was obliged to return to Pondicherry, where the Count de Lally required his assistance; and after the departure of "the guardian angel of my life and fortune," as the Nizam called the gallant French captain, Salabat Jung was dethroned by his brother Nizam Ali Khan—the ally of the English—and confined in the fort of Bidar, where he died in 1762.

Nizam Ali Khan was the first Nizam who made a treaty with the English. In 1766 he ceded to them the Northern Circars, on condition that he was to be furnished with a subsidiary force in time of war, and should receive six lakhs of rupees annually when no troops were required, he, on his part, promising to assist the British with his troops when called upon to do so. Further treaties were made between the Nizam and the British in 1768, in 1790, and in 1798, when the subsidiary troops were augmented and the Ceded Districts of Madras were made over to the English by the Nizam for the payment of the troops, including the famous Hyderabad Contingent, which had been formed in 1709 by Mir Alum.

Nizam Ali Khan died in 1803, and was succeeded by his son Sikandar Jah, who died in 1829, and was succeeded by his son Nasir-ud-Daula.

Nasir-ud-Daula was a humane and broad-minded ruler, and much beloved by his subjects. He was six feet three inches high, and possessed great bodily strength and a handsome appearance. But he was wanting in energy and ability, and towards the close of his reign he became very self-indulgent. In 1853, the payment of the Contingent troops having fallen into arrears, he made a treaty with the English by which the Districts of Berar, Osmanabad, and the Raichur

Doab were ceded to the British, and he pawned his jewels, which were taken to England. In May 1857, just at the commencement of the Mutiny, he died; and on his death-bed he told his son and successor, Afzul-ud-Daula, that as the British had always been friendly to the Nizams, so he should continue to be faithful to the English.

Nizam Afzul-ud-Daula followed his father's advice, and all through the terrible days of the Mutiny, he, and his minister, Sir Salar Jung I, stood by the English, thus preventing the Mutiny from spreading into southern India. In 1858 "Our Faithful Ally" received the thanks of the British Government, and a new treaty was then made between the Nizam and the English by which Osmanabad and the Raichur Doab Districts were restored to the Nizam, the assigned District of Berar being taken in trust by the British Government for the purposes specified in the treaty of 1853. (In November 1902 the assigned District of Berar was leased in perpetuity to the British Government at an annual rental of twenty-five lakhs of rupees.)

In 1869 Afzul-ud-Daula died and he was succeeded by his son, Mir Mahabub Ali Khan, who was then only three years old.

Sir Salar Jung I and Nawab Shams-ul-Umara were made co-regents, the advice of the British Resident being taken on all important matters, and the Regency continued until 1884, when His Highness was invested with sovereign rights and the full enjoyment of an annual income of some ten millions of rupees derived from *Sarf-i-khas* (crown) lands, to say nothing of crown jewels and precious stones, that are said to be priceless.

During the reign of H. H. Nizam Mir Mahabub Ali Khan many improvements were introduced into the State, and the changes brought about by Sir Salar Jung I were further developed. In 1893 the Cabinet and Legislative Councils were formed, and in the latter Council, for the first time in the annals of Hyderabad, the non-official element was allowed a voice in the work of administration, a privilege that has *not*, so far, been appreciated or developed by His Highness's subjects.

Education received much encouragement, the valuable State Library was opened, the Guaranteed State Railway became a paying concern, three large spinning and weaving mills and many small ginning and pressing factories came into existence, the Singareni coal fields were developed, and municipal government was fostered in the city and in the suburb of Chadarghat, and was introduced in the form of Local Boards and Local Funds into the Districts. The good work done during the long reign of H. H. Mir Mahabub Ali Khan will be seen in the following chapters, including the changes made in the four Divisions and the sixteen Districts into which the State was re-divided in 1905, the introduction of up-to-date machinery into the State Mint about the same time, and many kindred matters.

His Highness Mir Mahabub Ali Khan died in 1911, and was buried in the Cathedral Mosque in Hyderabad city amid the lamentations of his subjects. He was succeeded by H. H. Mir Osman Ali Khan Bahadur, who, if he lives, will (I quote the words of one of his Ministers) do more for Hyderabad than any Nizam has done before him.

THE NIZAMS.

Mir Kamar-ud-din, Nizam-ul-Mulk, Asaf Jah ..	1712—1748
Mir Ahmed Khan, Nasir Jung	1748—1750

Muzaffar Jung	.. ..	1750—1751
Salabat Jung	.. ..	1751—1761
Ali Khan	.. ..	1762—1803
Sikandar Jah	.. ..	1803—1829
Nasir-ud-Daula	.. ..	1829—1857
Afzul-ud-Daula	.. ..	1857—1869
Mir Mahabub Ali Khan	..	1869—1911
Mir Osman Ali Khan	..	1911—

THE MINISTERS.

Raja Rajunath Das	..	1750—1752
Nawab Lashka Khan	..	1752—1755
Nawab Shah Nawaz Khan	..	1755—1758
Nawab Basalut Jung	..	1758—1760
Raja Partabwunt ..	..	1761—1763
Nawab Rukum-ud-Daula	..	1765—1775

After the powerful Rukum-ud-Daula came the joint ministers Nawab Vikar-ud-Daula and Nawab Samsam-ul-Mulk; and the former was afterwards appointed sole minister. When the next minister, Aristo Jah, assumed office is not certain, but he was Minister in 1797 and remained so until he died in 1804.

Nawab Mir Alum (grand-father of Sir Salar Jung I)	..	1804—1808
Munir-ul-Mulk ..	..	1809—1832
Raja Chander Lal ..	..	1832—1843

Raja Ram Baksh ..	..	1843—1846
Nawab Siraj-ul-Mulk	..	1846—1848
Amjud-ul-Mulk ..	..	1848—1848
Nawab Shams-ul-Umara	..	1848—1849
Raja Ram Baksh ..	..	1849—1851
Ganesh Rao ..	..	1851—1851
Nawab Seraj-ul-Mulk	..	1851—1853
Sir Salar Jung I ..	..	1853—1858
Sir Salar Jung II ..	..	1884—1886
Sir Asman Jah ..	..	1887—1894
Sir Vikar-ul-Umara	..	1894—1901
Maharaja Sir Kishen Pershad	..	1901—1912
Nawab Salar Jung III	..	1912—

CHAPTER IV.

Sir Salar Jung I, and H. E. the Minister, Nawab Salar Jung Bahadur III.

No one can form an opinion on modern Hyderabad and appreciate its present condition without studying the life of that remarkable man, Sir Salar Jung I.

Here it will only be possible to give an idea of the manner in which he planted and watered the present administration, and started and fostered the institutions that now form an integral part of His Highness the Nizam's Government.

Moulvi Cheragh Ali says :—" Before the administration of H. E. the Nawab Salar Jung I there was no regular or systematic form of government, nor were there any separate departments of administration. Everything was in the hands of the Diwan or Minister, without any regular form of administration. It was altogether a new idea, an element foreign to the conservative mind of Hyderabad to have anything like an organised system of government."

That was only about sixty years ago, and when we see what has been done in Hyderabad during the last half century and watch the progress that is now being made, we cannot fail to feel hopeful concerning the future of the largest native State in India.

Mir Turab Ali Khan Bahadur, known as Sir Salar Jung I, was born in 1828, and the condition of Hyderabad at the time of his birth is thus described by Sir John Kaye, in his "Life of Lord Metcalfe":—

"The whole system of administration was rotten to the very core, it was a congeries of diseases. Nothing seemed to flourish there except corruption. Every man was bent on enriching himself at the expense of his neighbour. No one cared for the people, no one cared for the State. Everything had its price in Hyderabad. If a man wanted a place he counted out his money to buy it. If a man wanted justice, he bade for it as for any other marketable commodity. Every public office, in every department of the State, was accessible to a bribe . . . Neither life nor property was secure . . . There was nothing left indeed but the name of government, all the rest was lawlessness and confusion."

In 1853 the Minister, Nawab Seraj-ul-Mulk, died; and his nephew, Nawab Salar Jung, who was then only twenty-five years old, was chosen by Nizam Nasir-ud-Daula to succeed him.

Nizam Nasir-ud-Daula was then nearing the close of his reign, and, owing to self-indulgence, he was surrounded by flatterers and plunderers. He had crippled the finances of the State by ceding Berar, Osmanabad, and the Raichur Doab to the English, and had even pawned his jewels, which had been taken by Mr. Dighton to England. The revenue, the administration, the treasury, and the credit of the State were all in a deplorable condition when Nawab Salar Jung I became Minister, but he wrote to Mr. Dighton:—"I shall, nevertheless, do my best, with God's help, to restore order in the affairs of this country, and endeavour to extricate the government from its embarrassments."

He had no personal influence with the Nizam, and in 1853 (the year he became Minister) he wrote to Colonel Low:—"You are aware that Burhan-ud-Din is my medium of communication with the Nizam, and he is the only man who has influence enough with His Highness to persuade him to consent to my measures." He appealed in this letter for the support of the Governor-General, in a way that showed his confidence in receiving from the English the help he could not obtain from his royal master.

In 1857 Nasir-ud-Daula died, and was succeeded by his son Afzal-ud-Daula, and history does not show that any great reforms were introduced into Hyderabad before 1859 —two years after the Mutiny. Then, if "Our Faithful Ally" took no active part in State affairs, he did not, at any rate, interfere with the work of his Minister, and Nawab Salar Jung I was allowed to proceed with his reforms, and may-be he received from the Nizam help and encouragement.

It is not possible to give here a complete list of the changes made and the institutions introduced, but among them were a Central Treasury and a State Bank in Hyderabad city, a Board of Revenue for the purpose of supervising the revenue administration of the country, and a system of police for the districts.

The following lands were then defined: *Sarf-i-khas* (crown) lands; *Paigah* (Paigah means "stable," and these lands were originally given for the maintenance of a body of horse called His Highness' Household troops) lands; *Jagir* (a form of land tenure common among Mahomedans and dating back to the earliest times) lands; and *Khalsa* or Government lands.

In 1867 the State was divided into five Divisions and seventeen Districts, and Subedars, or Governors, were appointed for the five Divisions and talukdars and tehsildars for the districts.

The Judicial, Public Works, Medical, Educational, Municipal, and Police Departments were re-organised.

And in 1868 *Sadr-ul-Mahams* or Assistant Ministers were appointed for the Judicial, Revenue, Police, and Miscellaneous Departments.

In 1869 Nizam Afzul-ud-Daula died, and was succeeded by his infant son Mir Mahabub Ali Khan, and Sir Salar Jung I was then appointed co-regent with Nawab Shams-ul-Umara, an appointment he filled until the day of his death, acting for a portion of the time as sole Regent.

Writing in 1869, Mr. Saunders, the British Resident, bore eloquent testimony to the changes introduced during the reign of Nizam Afzul-ud-Daula, and said that

Hyderabad of 1869 was as unlike the Hyderabad of 1820 as England of even date was unlike the England of the Stuarts.

In Elphinstone's history is an interesting account of Sir Salar Jung's daily life.

He rose at 6 A.M., took a cup of tea and proceeded to hold a public durbar, at which the poorest of the people had opportunities to make their representations. The officers of the troops then made their reports and afterwards he went to his private rooms, where he inspected treasury receipts and attended to correspondence. The *Nazim* (Dispenser of Justice) then had an audience. At 10-30 A.M. he had breakfast, which lasted for about fifteen minutes. Afterwards he was engaged in miscellaneous business until 12-30 A.M., when he held a second public durbar and granted private interviews and attended to Residency business. After a short siesta and afternoon prayers he received the officers of the Government, bankers, local governors and others. At 5-30 P.M. he walked, rode, or drove and inspected his horses. After dinner and evening prayers he attended to his correspondence and at 10 P.M. he went to bed.

Sir Salar Jung I died on the 5th of February 1883, and was buried in the family burial place, in the Daira Mir Momin Cemetery, in Hyderabad city, which place he is said to have called "the real home of our race." A simple stone grave, without name or inscription, marks his last resting place, and beside him lies his son and successor, Sir Salar Jung II, and near by is the grave of his illustrious ancestor, Mir Alum.

His Excellency the Minister, NAWAB MIR YOUSUF ALI KHAN BAHADUR.

Salar Jung Bahadur III, the present Prime Minister of Hyderabad, was born in June 1889, and he was only one month old when his father, Sir Salar Jung II, died. At school he had a brilliant career, and showed resolution and firmness of character, and since that time a great resemblance has been found between him and his famous grandfather. In March 1912 H. H. the Nizam invested him with full administrative power over his large estates, which comprise an area of 1,480 square miles and the revenues of which amount to nearly twelve lakhs of rupees a year. And on July 11th, 1912, His Highness appointed him Prime Minister, the following firman being issued the same day:

"As Maharaja Sir Kishen Pershad Bahadur has applied for six months' leave of absence and has expressed his desire to be relieved of the responsibilities of Prime Minister, it is hereby ordered that six months' leave has been granted to him and that he has been relieved of the duties of Prime Minister, but he will continue to be Peshkar as usual. Nawab Salar Jung Bahadur has been appointed officiating Prime Minister for the present and on probation for three years or until fresh orders issue. In order to enable him to discharge the responsible duties of this high office expeditiously and obtain experience therein, Nawab Imud-ul-Mulk, C.S.I., has been appointed, until fresh orders, his Special Adviser, that he may help and advise him. The officiating Prime Minister will have all the powers that have been conferred on the permanent Prime Minister by the Khanooncha and the Regulations framed thereunder and the orders in force from time to time. All noblemen, jagirdars, officers and subjects, and other residents are hereby enjoined to obey and fully carry out the orders of the officiating Prime Minister, Nawab Salar Jung Bahadur."*

* On the 20th of July, 1914, His Excellency was confirmed in his high office by His Highness the Nizam, and Hyderabadis hope and pray that before him may lie a long career, for he is extremely popular.

Speaking that evening at a banquet given by H. H. the Nizam at King Koti Palace, in celebration of his birthday anniversary, the British Resident, Colonel A. F. Pinhey, said :—

" Salar Jung ! What a name to conjure with in Hyderabad ! He has everything in his favour to start with, youth, an historical and honoured name, and an unblemished character. I see no reason why he should not meet with as much success or even more than his illustrious grandfather, and in congratulating him, we can, at the same time, congratulate His Highness on the wise and popular choice which he has made."

His Excellency Nawab Salar Jung Bahadur III has now held the office of Prime Minister for more than two years, and those who know him well speak of his tact, patience, integrity, and ability in all that concerns State business. His charm of manner and artistic tastes make him a general favourite, and it is believed that when the time comes for him to stand alone, he will be found to possess all the qualities that in a Prime Minister make for usefulness and greatness.

CHAPTER V.

THE ADMINISTRATION TO-DAY.

The area of the Hyderabad State is 82,698 square miles, and the land is thus divided:

Sarf-i-khas, or crown land, which is privately owned by H. H. the Nizam.

Paigah land, belonging to the descendants of the late Sir Asman Jah, Sir Khurshed Jah, and Sir Vikar-ul-Umara, a sort of feudal tenure for the maintenance of troops for the Nizam's service.

Jagir land. Gifts of land made by former Nizams as royal gifts, or for the support of troops for the Nizam's use.

Khalsa, or government land.

The *Sarf-i-khas*, *Paigah*, and *Jagir* lands make up one-third of the whole area of the State, and in speaking of the administration, revenue, etc., it must be clearly understood that only the *Khalsa* or Government land is referred to in this book.

And it must not be forgotten that a Nizam is in his State absolute.

So far the present ruler has shewn no inclination to interfere with government revenue, which pays for the administration, the Courts of Justice, the State army, the Public Service, etc. His Highness is much too intelligent and enlightened a ruler to jeopardise the good government of the State, the loyalty of his subjects, and the good-will of the Government of India by such a course of conduct. With other Nizams it has, however, been different; and it is well to bear in mind that the powers of the ruler of Hyderabad are almost limitless, not only as regards *Paigah* and *Jagir* lands, where he can give or take away as he pleases, and *Sarf-i-khas* lands, which he rules as a private landlord, but also concerning the lands and the revenue of the government. His Highness can, and does, banish from his Dominions such persons as seem to him to be undesirable residents; he appoints guardians and directors for his young nobles; and if a *Jagirdar* is oppressing the ryots, he suspends or deposes the offender. But he does not touch what may be called "public monies," although he is cognisant and gives his consent to all that is done with them. He receives yearly from the government revenue

O. S. rupees 50,00,000 (since he came to the *gadi* the Halli Sicca rupee has been re-named, and it is now called the Osmania Sicca rupee) as " stipends and allowances ; " and State receptions and entertainments are paid for out of government funds. He is probably the wealthiest man in India, for the *Sarf-i-khas* lands include the city of Hyderabad and the *Atraf-i-balda*, or suburbs of the city, and he has shooting preserves that remind us of the days of William Rufus.

In order to appreciate the true position of H. H. the Nizam, let us imagine the Governor of the Madras Presidency holding a life appointment, and having for his private use the customs of the city of Madras and its suburbs, absolute control over the ruling chiefs, rajas and zemindars in Southern India, and the power to appropriate the whole of the Madras Presidency, which (the Coromandel coast and Coimbatore being excluded) is of the same size as H. H. the Nizam's Dominions.

History shows that sometimes Viceroys and Governors in British India have been inflated by the limited and constitutional powers that they possess ; and if we would judge such a ruler as a Nizam justly, then we must not forget that he wields the powers enjoyed by Richard the Second of England, and the Government of India is to him very much what the Pope was to that impulsive monarch.

The following description of His Highness's powers as regards government affairs is taken from an administration report written by Maharaja Sir Kishen Pershad Bahadur while he was Prime Minister.

"The administrative control of all State affairs is understood to rest with His Excellency the Minister, but in actual practice no action involving consequences of an important and permanent character is taken without the knowledge of His Highness, and his command is alone final in the last resort. No new law or regulation can be introduced, and no existing law or regulation can be altered, without the sanction of His Highness. No grant can be made of State lands or of any recurring allowance from State funds, no transfer of any existing State grant in lands or cash, either by inheritance or sale, mortgage or gift, can be made otherwise than with the permission of His Highness. No fresh expenditure of a recurring or unusual character can be made from State funds, no loan can be granted from the government treasury, no fresh tax or impost can be introduced otherwise than with His Highness's sanction. The same authority is needed for creating any new post in government service, carrying a salary of more than Rs. 500. No European can be appointed to the State service, nor can any one be granted the rank of commissioned officer in the State army, without His Highness's permission. Death sentences can be carried out only after the confirmation of the Nizam."

This was written while His Highness the late Nizam was on the *gadi*, and it is only necessary to add that the present ruler of Hyderabad has made himself intimately acquainted with the working of each State department, that he has a thirst for public affairs, and that he shews a determination to master every detail of government business. But he relies on the advice of those who have spent many years in the government service, and when His Excellency Nawab Salar Jung III was made Prime Minister, he appointed as Special Adviser to His Excellency one of his own earliest tutors, Nawab Imud-ul-Mulk Bahadur, and continued in his position as Political Secretary to Government and Private Secretary to H. E. the Minister, Nawab Faridoon Jung Bahadur, who is, no doubt, a great diplomatist.

And this is an appropriate place, I think, in which to briefly describe the two remarkable men who have played such important parts in the administration of the Hyderabad State during the past two years.

NAWAB IMUD-UL-MULK BAHADUR, C.S.I. The family of Nawab Imud-ul-Mulk Bahadur is said to have come to India about 1217 A.D., with Muhammad Ghori, the Afghan conqueror, and to have settled in Oudh. His father was deputy collector and deputy magistrate in various parts of Bengal and Behar. He was born at Gya, in 1844, and after being educated in various schools and colleges in Calcutta, where he graduated in the first class from the Hare Academy, he chose the educational service for his career, and he was appointed professor of Arabic in the Canning College at Lucknow.

When Sir Salar Jung visited Lucknow in 1872, that great statesman perceived the possibilities of the young professor of Arabic, and offered him an appointment in Hyderabad. Thither he went in 1873, and ever since his life has been devoted to the State, his adopted home. In 1876 he accompanied Sir Salar Jung to England, and on his return to Hyderabad, he was appointed Private Secretary to His Excellency the Minister and Secretary to Government in the Miscellaneous Department, which had, among other things, control over State education. From that time the education of both sexes absorbed much of his attention, and he set himself the task of adapting "all that is best in Western education to the needs of an Eastern people." To the teachers under his control, he gave the motto "kindness and discipline," and so highly did H. H. the late Nizam think of him as an educationist that he was appointed one of the earliest tutors of the present ruler.

At this time he compiled with Mr. M. C. Wilmott an "*Historical and Descriptive Sketch of the Nizam's Dominions;*" and shortly after the death of Sir Salar Jung I, he wrote a biography of that great man. He was, afterwards, much sought after to fill public appointments outside Hyderabad State, as well as in it. In 1900 he presided over the Mahomedan Educational Conference, and later he was selected as a member of the Universities Commission, which had for its object "an attempt to discover a remedy for the evils that had arisen in British India from grafting a Western education upon an Eastern people." He was then chosen by Lord Curzon to serve on the Imperial Legislative Council, and in 1907 he was appointed the first Mahomedan Member of the Council of the Secretary of State for India. In 1908 he was made a Companion of the Star of India, and it was believed that he would do much good for his co-religionists in London. But the English climate did not suit his health and he returned to Hyderabad, where, after the sad and unexpected death of H. H. Mir Mahabub Ali Khan, he was appointed Special Adviser to H. E. the Minister, Nawab Salar Jung Bahadur III, a position he held until his retirement on the 20th of July, 1914.

Nawab Imud-ul-Mulk Bahadur is by nature and inclination a scholar. He prefers a simple and retired life. But has never failed to come forward when needed and to give his time, talents, and great experience to H. H. the Nizam and to the people of his adopted land. To-day he is busy with his *magnum opus*, a translation of the Koran into English. He objects to publicity of any sort, but his important position and distinguished career render it necessary that some record of his life should be written, and we can only hope that when this appears, it will do him justice.

NAWAB FARIDOON JUNG BAHADUR, C.S.I., C.I.E., Political Secretary to Government and Private Secretary to H. E. the Minister.

Nawab Faridoon Jung Bahadur is, perhaps, the most interesting person in H. H. the Nizam's Dominions. Born in the Aurangabad District, in September 1849, he has risen through the various grades of the Government service to the unique position that he holds to-day. He has served under six administrations and has acted as Private Secretary to five Prime Ministers—Sir Salar Jung II, Sir Asman Jah, Sir Vikar-ul-Umara, Maharaja Sir Kishen Pershad Bahadur, and H. E. Nawab Salar Jung Bahadur III. Shrewdness, tact, commonsense, politeness, loyalty, and patience seem to be his chief characteristics. From intrigue of every sort he has always held aloof, and, in consequence, he has received the confidence of two Nizams and of five successive Prime

Ministers. An easy and somewhat cynical nonchalance characterises him; and being kind-hearted and courteous, he has made many friends and few enemies during the long period that he has held his important office. The knowledge of the State and State affairs that Nawab Faridoon Jung possesses to-day makes him invaluable to H. H. the Nizam and to His Highness's Government, and his marvellous capacity to say and do the right thing on the spur of the moment—well to few do the gods give these gifts in such a happy combination.

As the friend and admirer of England, Nawab Faridoon Jung is an Imperial asset; and the link he makes between the Mahomedans and the English in Hyderabad and Secunderabad prevents friction or misunderstanding. In recognition of his valuable services to the Hyderabad State, the British Government has conferred on him the distinction of being a Companion of the Order of the Star of India and of the Indian Empire. He is at present one of the most trusted councillors of the Nizam, and the leading statesman in Hyderabad, as well as the most influential of His Highness the Nizam's subjects.

As regards the administration, I will continue to quote from the administration report of Maharaja Sir Kishen Pershad Bahadur :—

"The Political Department, including all correspondence between the Hon'ble the Resident and His Highness's Government, is in the charge of the Minister, and in this department all dealings between the Government of India and His Highness the Nizam's Government are carried on. The Minister is assisted in the work of administration by four assistant ministers, who administer, subject to his control, the various departments entrusted to their charge. The powers of the assistant ministers are strictly limited by rule, and their orders, for the most part, require to be confirmed by the Minister before they can take effect. The assistant ministers have charge of the judicial, the military, the financial and the miscellaneous departments.

The revenue department is directly under the Minister and is controlled by a Director-General.

The departmental secretaries, who have been called " the pivot of the administration in Hyderabad State" hold positions of great importance, and are in charge of the financial, revenue, judicial, public works, and military secretariats.

THE CABINET COUNCIL. In 1893 A.D. the consultative body known as the Cabinet Council was added to the institutions of the State. Its President is the Minister, and its members are the assistant ministers. This Council was formed chiefly to assist and advise the Minister in matters of State administration, and it lies in his discretion to refer to it for deliberation any proposal upon which he desires the Council's advice. Also, any assistant minister has the right of asking that any proposal of his may be laid before the Cabinet Council, though the Minister has the right of refusal, subject to His Highness's final commands.

In addition, certain classes of business have been specially reserved for the consideration of the Council, such as the annual State Budget of accounts, final disposal of cases for the report on which special commissions have been appointed, questions relating to State concessions, and important questions arising out of the proceedings of the Legislative Council, and any other matters which from time to time are declared fit subjects for the Council's deliberations.

The President of the Council (His Excellency the Minister) has the right of overruling any decision arrived at by a majority of the Council, in anticipation of His Highness's sanction.

The Legislative Council was established in 1893 A.D.

The Council is composed of a President, a Vice-President, and seventeen members. The Minister is the President, and the assistant minister of the department, in connection with which any Bill may be under the consideration of the Council, acts as Vice-President during the discussion of such Bill. Of the members, three are *ex-officio*, namely, the Chief Justice of the Hyderabad High Court, the judicial secretary to government, and the legal adviser. The remaining fourteen are appointed by the Minister for a space of two years at a time, but any of them is eligible for re-appointment at the end of that period. Of these, eight are government officials and six are non-officials. Two of the non-official members must be holders of jagirs or other hereditary rights, free from encumbrances, and yielding a net annual income of Rs. 6,000 and must be selected by the holders of such jagirs or rights in the State, from amongst their number. The other members must be similarly elected by the High Court pleaders from amongst themselves. Of the remaining two non-official members one must be chosen from each of the three *Paigah Illakas* by turn and one from the general public.

The legal adviser, besides being a member, acts as the secretary of the Council.

No bill or motion affecting the public revenues, or the religion of any class of His Highness's subjects, or the organisation and discipline of His Highness's troops, or the relation of His Highness's Government with the British Government, or the Act relating to the Legislative Council, can be introduced without the previous permission of the Minister. Other bills passed by the Council and approved by the Minister can come into force at once. His Highness, however, has the right to order the repeal or amendment of any enactment. In undertaking any legislative measure, the Council is bound to be guided by the principles of Mahomedan law, the tenets of the Hindu shastras, the special laws of every community residing in His Highness's Dominions, the customs and usages having the force of law and the jurisprudence of British India or other civilised countries. No Act of the Council, nor any power granted to it, can in any way affect the rights and prerogatives of His Highness as the supreme ruler of the State.

THE FOUR DIVISIONS OF THE STATE. For administrative purposes, the State is divided into four divisions—Aurangabad, Medak, Gulbarga, and Warangal—and each division is under a revenue commissioner, called the "Subedar." The divisions are further divided into sixteen districts, including the *Sarf-i-khas* district, and each district is under a magistrate or collector, called a talukdar. The districts are sub-divided into talukas and tahsils, each under a sub-divisional officer, called second or third talukdar, according to his grade in the service; and two or three talukas are placed under a tahsildar. And each village has its patel or head man. More will be said concerning these matters later on.

CHAPTER VI.

THE LAND.

Natural Divisions.

The Census for Hyderabad State, published this year, says :—" While in relation to those of the Indian continent the geological and meteorological characters of the Deccan plateau (the Nizam's Dominions are situated almost in the centre of the Deccan tableland) are sufficiently distinctive to constitute a single natural division. Taken by itself they fall naturally into two groups dividing the area into two natural divisions."

And the Report of the Census of India, 1901, says :—" The north-west portion, forming nearly half of the natural division, is covered with basaltic lava flows (Deccan trap) ; the remainder is composed of granites, gneisses, and schists with a basin of Paleozoic limestones, quartzites, and igneous rocks in the Caddapah area. The dry season extends from December to May. The rainfall of the wet season is chiefly due to the West Coast humid current from June to August, but occasionally in September and almost entirely in October and November it accompanies the course of storms coming up from the Bay of Bengal. The wet season is hence considerably longer than in the Konkan and usually lasts until the middle of November. As the rainfall in the large area of the west Deccan is less than 30 inches "the dry zone of the division is very liable to drought and famine."

These observations describe exactly the geological and meteorological differences between the western and eastern halves of the Nizam's Dominions.

The division to the north-west is a trappean or black cotton soil country—a land of wheat and cotton, while the division to the south-east is a granitic region—a land of tanks and rice.

"These differences of physical nature are associated," says the Census, "with social, economic, and linguistic differences in the two natural divisions of the State, which are designated as Marathwara and Telingana, owing to Marathi and Telegu being the principal languages spoken in these two tracts respectively."

And here it will be useful to give the following figures: Hyderabad State: Area, 82,698 sq. miles. Population, 13,374,676. Density per sq. mile, 162. Telingana division: Area in sq. miles, 41,320. Population, 6,724,964. Density per sq. mile, 163. Marathwara division: Area in sq. miles, 41,378. Population, 6,649,712. Density per sq. mile, 161.

Thus it will be seen that His Highness's Dominions are not very densely populated when compared with other parts of India, a fact worth noticing, because density of population has, no doubt, much to do with unrest and discontent among Indians.

When I asked a Hindu in the Warangal division why people appear to be more contented in the Hyderabad State than in British India, he replied:—"Because they are not so crowded."

The following figures as regards density of population are of interest:—

Presidency of Bengal: Area in sq. miles, including Cooch Behar and Hill Tippera, 84,092 sq. miles. Population, 46,305,642 persons. Density per sq. mile, 551.

Presidency of Bombay: Area in sq. miles, 186,923. Population, 27,084,317 persons. Density to the sq. mile, 145.

Mysore State: Area in sq. miles, 29,475. Population, 5,806,193 persons. Density to sq. mile, 197.

Travancore State: Area in sq. miles, 7,594. Population, 3,428,975. Density to sq. mile, 452.

Bearing in mind the two natural divisions of the State that are very strongly marked and must impress anyone who travels in the districts, we notice with interest that of the whole forest area in the Nizam's Dominions—18,000 sq. miles—no less than 16,000 sq. miles are in Telingana. Yet, owing to the cultivation of rice, the density of population is greater in Telingana than in Marathwara. This division has a better rainfall than Marathwara, but the ryot in Telingana is less painstaking than in the sister division. The Marathwara ryot is hard-working and industrious, and although irrigation is inconsiderable in his division, he is blessed with a soil that is retentive of moisture and in which his principal cereal crop—wheat—will flourish. And it must be noticed that although rice and wheat—and more especially rice—occupy in the agricultural industries of the State a position of importance unapproached by any other crops, jowari, bajri, and cotton cover a larger area.

The following figures are important:—

State of Hyderabad: Percentage of total area cultivated 53·7. Ditto of cultivated area which is irrigated 6·2. Under rice 4·4. Wheat 3·7. Pulses 7·4. Other crops 84·5. Normal rainfall 30·2 inches.

Telingana: Percentage of total area cultivated 38·8. Ditto of cultivated area that is irrigated 13·0. Rice 10·3. Wheat 0·4. Pulses 5·5. Other crops 83·8. Normal rainfall 32·7 inches.

Marathwara: Percentage of total area cultivated 68·6. Ditto of cultivated area that is irrigated 2·4. Rice 1·1. Wheat 5·5. Pulses 11·1. Other crops 82·0. Rainfall 27·7 inches.

The Census tells us that during the past decade Telingana has increased in wealth and population, while Marathwara has decreased as regards prosperity and inhabitants, and it suggests that in the Census for 1911 the wild and nomadic tribes in the forest districts of Telingana have been more accurately enumerated than was the case in 1901. Large tracts of land have been reclaimed from the jungle in Telingana during late years, and that division has suffered less from drought, plague, and famine than Marathwara. While the percentage of increase of population during the past ten years has been in Telingana 24·0, in Marathwara it has been only 16·4. The writers of the special articles that are printed with the Census are of opinion that practically all the cultivated area in Marathwara has now come under cultivation, and that this division is already supporting a population much nearer to the maximum capacity of its agriculture than Telingana.

Rice cultivation, which has the capacity to support a proportionately larger population than that of any other crop, is inconsiderable in Marathwara, and the scanty and uncertain rainfall there is opposed to a rapid growth of population. Large areas, and, as a rule, the more fertile ones, have been transferred to the production of non-food crops, which bring higher prices. Between the years 1902 and 1910, the area under cotton in the State increased by 21 per cent., and most of this cotton land is in Marathwara.

The Census suggests the substitution of more paying crops, improved methods of cultivation, and the establishment of new industries, but it says nothing about more money being spent on roads and irrigation works.

The soils of the two divisions are very different. Those of Telingana are sandy, the plains there are covered with brushwood, the hills show no vegetation, and fantastic-shaped rocks and crags give to the scenery a wild and, in some places, weird appearance. The rivers run dry in the hot weather, and if water were not stored in tanks, little or no agriculture could be carried on. There are five crops, but the light soil requires little ploughing and harrowing, and rice seems to be the only crop to which the cultivator pays much attention. The principal crops are rice, jowari, bajri, castor-oil seed, sesame, and pulses; and the ryots live on rice, jowari, and bajri—also goat flesh.

The Marathwara soil is very fertile—heavy and rich in the hilly parts and light and loamy in the valleys. Two crops only are raised. The Marathwara ryot weeds his wheat, cotton, linseed, and pulses crops carefully, and his food is bajri, jowari and wheat, varied with fish and goat flesh. Strong ploughs and harrows are used in Marathwara, and the work to be done in the fields is heavy and constant.

Rather more than one-half of the population of the State is supported by agriculture, and the Census gives the following figures as regards the cultivators of the soil:—

Rent receivers	..	731,803
Ordinary cultivators	..	4,064,950
Agents, managers, etc.	..	34,540
Farm servants and farm labourers ..	..	2,788,212

There has, during the past ten years, been an extraordinary increase in the number of rent receivers, the Census says, and this shows that the pressure on the land is increasing, and the ownership and profits thereof are being increasingly appropriated by rent receivers. The number of farm labourers and field servants has been swollen by peasant proprietors who have lost their holdings and by indigenous artizans thrown out of employment by cheaper imported articles. The bania, or money-lender, seems to be increasing in power in the Nizam's Dominions, as well as in other parts of India.

Concerning the wages received by farm servants and farm labourers, nothing definite is known, because such people are largely paid in kind, and are more or less the slaves of the cultivators. "To sell into slavery" is a criminal offence in Hyderabad State, but there is no doubt that in remote places farm labourers still sometimes sell their children to their employers, and sometimes bind themselves to work for a certain number of years, and even for a life-time in return for money given to defray marriage expenses, and little girls are sometimes bartered for food, clothes, and sandals.

The common system of land tenure all over the State is *ryotwari*, and by this system each field is considered a holding, and the right of occupancy depends on the regular payment of the assessment. Non-payment of rent means forfeiture of the right to the land, which is then sold to pay the arrears.

If the rent is paid regularly, the ryot, although the period of holding is nominally for one year only, retains his land indefinitely. He may sell, sub-let, or transfer his right to the land and relinquish his holding by giving due notice.

The Imperial Gazetteer of India, Hyderabad State (Provincial Series), says :—

"The average area of a holding in the whole State is 20¾ acres, varying from 28½ acres in Marathwara to 12½ acres in Telingana. In the Maratha districts the government assessment on 'dry' lands ranges from Rs. 3-0-1 to Re. 0-10-2 per acre, the average being Re. 0-12-9, while for 'wet' and *baghat* (garden) lands the average is Rs. 4-5-6 per acre, the maximum being Rs. 15 and the minimum Re. 1-2-0. In the Telingana districts the average assessment on 'dry' lands is Re. 0-13-5 (maximum Rs. 4, minimum Re. 0-1-0) and on 'wet' lands Rs. 9-4-2, the maximum and minimum being Rs. 24 and Rs. 3 respectively. The average rate per acre for the whole State is Re. 1-3-8, but for Marathwara and Telingana it is Re. 0-14-3 and Re. 1-13-10 respectively, the high rate of assessment and the smallness of holdings in Telingana being due to the prevalence of 'wet' cultivation. No reliable figures are available to show the gross produce, and it is impossible to say what proportion of the land revenue demand bears to it. No difficulty is experienced in collecting the revenue, and there is very little resort to coercive measures. The general principle of assessment is to take half the net profits, after paying cost of cultivation, etc., as the State's share."

In times of scarcity and famine the demand is suspended and recovered in the following year, and remissions are also granted when distress is severe or when the ryot has lost his cattle. In Marathwara and in the settled Telingana districts, remissions are not granted for "dry" land, as the assessment is very light. But in the unsettled Telingana districts, remissions are given on "dry" lands affected by bad seasons, including excessive rain, and on "wet" lands for want of water, including breach of tanks and decay of wells. These remissions are granted in ordinary years. Remissions are also given for "wet" lands in settled districts when the water supply fails.

The land revenue derived by His Highness's government from *khalsa* or government lands (two-thirds of the State) was, according to the administration report for the two years 1320-21 Fasli (1910-1912 A.D.) 4,92,45,280 O.S. rupees; and during the same period the total cultivated area rose from 19,216,662 acres to 20,261,443 acres.

The State, which is an extensive plateau, has an average elevation of about 1,250 feet above the level of the sea, and summits rising here and there to 2,000 and 3,500 feet. The principal mountains are the Balaghat, the Sahyadriparvat, the Jalna, and the Kandikal Gutta ranges, but there is no hill resort, and the chief sanatorium of the State is at Bolarum in the Secunderabad cantonment.

The principal rivers are the Godavari and the Kistna, with their tributaries the Tungabhada, the Purna, the Manjra, the Bhima and the Maner; and among the smaller rivers are the Musi—a dangerous stream that flows below the wall of Hyderabad city—the Windi and the Munair.

Gold and diamonds are still found in the State, but mining for these things has not proved a success of late years. The only gold mine that is now being worked lies about fifty miles from Raichur, and is reached by a cart road. The output of gold at this mine—called the Hutti mine—was during 1912 16,993 ozs., and the royalty paid to His Highness's government during the same period was 48,110 B. G. rupees. Speaking of gold mines in the preface to his Budget Note for 1323 Fasli (1913-1914 A.D.) the Finance Minister says:—

"It is believed that as soon as railway communication enables the mining companies to get cheaper coal there will be a considerable extension of gold mining in the Deccan. There are many old workings in the Raichur district but none of these go down further than 700 feet. The experience of Mysore and of the Hutti mine in this State is the same, that the lower levels which the old workers never reached are the richest, but to reach these levels in the absence of railway communication is at present very expensive, and the industry has hitherto been unable to expand."

The Singareni coal fields will be noticed in a separate chapter.

Laminated limestone is largely quarried at Shahabad, in the Gulbarga district, and promises to become an important export.

The Nizam's Dominions abound with wild animals and feathered game, but the rules for shooting are very strict, and for full information concerning these things, the reader is referred to the monthly Directory published at the Garrison Military Printing Press, Secunderabad. Nowhere in India, except in Mysore, perhaps, will a greater variety of wild animals and birds be found.

The present Nizam is a keen sportsman, but so far he has been too much occupied with State affairs to spend much time in his large preserves.

CHAPTER VII.

THE PEOPLE.

ORDINARY persons in British India often express surprise when they hear that His Highness's subjects are nearly all Hindus and that the Mahomedans in Hyderabad State (given the area) scarcely exceed in number the English people in British India.

"But I thought that Hyderabad was a Mahomedan State!" such people say.

The total population of Hyderabad State was, in 1911 A.D., 13,374,676 people, and the distribution of the population as regards religion was then as follows:—

Hindus	..	11,626,146
Mahomedans	..	1,380,990
Animists	..	285,722
Christians	..	54,296
Jains	..	21,026

The Census says that during the last decade there has been a twenty per cent. increase of the total population, but the Hindu rate of increase has not kept pace with that of the population as a whole. It points out that the Christian missionaries have made many converts among the depressed classes during the past ten years, and estimates the Christian converts at 26,700 persons for that period. The missionaries would, no doubt, place the figures much higher, for they claim to make 7,000 converts each year in the Hyderabad State at the present time.

"No one, of course, returned himself as an animist," says the Census, "but all those who did not say that they professed any other religion, if they belonged to the Andh, Bhil, Erkula, Gond, and Lambada castes, have been classed in the Census of 1911 as animists"; and it goes on to explain that animism consists in the worship of inanimate objects, but the objects thus worshipped must not represent a higher power, because if so the worshippers could rightly be classed as Hindus. And as Hindus, no doubt, many of these so-called animists were entered in the Census of 1901.

Musalmans constitute the largest section of the population next to Hindus, and during the last ten years their numbers have slightly decreased in the districts, but have increased in Hyderabad city, where there are now exactly 100 more Musalmans in every 10,000 of the population than there were thirty years ago.

The new Census contains much interesting information concerning the birth rate. There is no excess, it says, of male births but more male than female infants die during the first year of their lives. After the fifth year is passed, the male population is in excess of the female, and women then remain in a position of numerical inferiority until the end. That the women do not live as long as the men in Hyderabad State is proved by the statistics; but it is difficult to obtain the correct ages of the women. "Every woman," says the Census, "who can possibly do so seems to have a fancy for returning herself as between twenty and twenty-five years of age." Early marriages are given as one cause of the higher mortality of females than males, and the fact that there are at the present time in the State 24,006 married females and 6,792 widows under ten years of age, and 27,913 married and 1,258 widows under five years of age, gives support to this statement, although, no doubt, in most cases the marriages are mere betrothals.

The hard manual labour done by Hindu women of the lower classes has probably much to do with the high rate of female mortality, also the unskilled midwifery, which the Victoria Zenana Hospital in Hyderabad is now trying to do away with. The proportion of female to male children has, however, increased during the last decade, for while in 1901 the male and female populations under ten years of age numbered 1,414,320 and 1,393,700, in 1911 they numbered 1,788,219 males and 1,830,461 females.

There are fewer females in Telingana than in Marathwara, although the proportion of early married women is highest in the latter division. And in Hyderabad city, owing to the large immigrant population, there are only 660 females per 1,000 males.

Mahomedan women marry later than their Hindu sisters and they appear to live longer, owing, no doubt, to the fact that the members of the ruling community are physically and materially better off than those of the subject races. Also Mahomedan women are very strictly secluded and are seldom, if ever, allowed to become "beasts of burden." Travel the State from end to end, and you will not find a Mahomedan woman showing her face, much less working in the fields and carrying on her back a load that would make a mule stagger and cause a pack-horse to show impatience.

The four principal languages of the State are Urdu—which is the official language—Telegu, Marathi and Canarese; and the people who talk these languages—96 per cent. of the population—are as follows:—

Telegu	.. ..	6,367,578
Marathi	.. ..	3,498,758
Canarese	.. ..	1,680,005
Urdu	.. ..	1,341,622

The number of people in the State who speak Urdu is much the same (according to the area) as of those who talk English in British India. There are many minor vernaculars, including the gypsy dialects. English is spoken by 8,843 persons, of whom 7,000 live in the capital and its suburbs. About 5,600 persons speak Arabic, and 256 talk and write Persian.

Agriculture supports 54 per cent. of the workers and their dependants, and 45 per cent. of the people are supported by the various industries of the State, such as the extraction of metals, cotton spinning and weaving, wood, food and building industries, and industries connected with trade and transport.

Only 28,377 persons—independent of rent receivers—live on their income, and no less than 22,852 persons of this class are in Hyderabad city and its suburbs. Outside the city area there is no leisured class, and in the city, owing to a reduction in the number of State pensioners, this class has largely decreased, for in the Census of 1901 they were entered as 51,757 persons.

The active part taken by women in the work of the State is shewn in the new Census. No less than 130,857 are rice pounders, huskers, etc. Women cultivate the land, breed animals, and help to make roads and bridges. They sell milk, butter, eggs, fowls, hay, grass, sweetmeats, betel leaf and cardamoms. They make tobacco, perfumery, toys, kites, baskets and pottery. They act as midwives, vaccinators, and dealers in precious stones, and (privately) they do a good deal of money-lending. A large number are entered in the Census as "ministers and priests," and no doubt the Christian missionaries help to swell this list, for, finding that their male converts lapse into heathenism unless they are married to Christian girls, the missionaries have now entered the matrimonial market, and educate large numbers of girls as Bible women and marry such girls to their male converts.

The Census says that the women of the State have a keen commercial instinct, and show a marked aptitude for business of all sorts. In the cotton mills and ginning and pressing factories women have found a new employment, and it is not uncommon now to see father, mother, and children all working in the same cotton factory, while the baby sleeps in a basket among the cotton fluff. And in the coal mines, at Singareni, women are employed, going down the shaft with the men miners and taking the same risks. And such women are always decently dressed, in fact some of the female miners go down the shaft with all their jewelry on them, including bracelets and anklets that must greatly hamper their movements.

CHAPTER VIII.

FINANCE.

FINANCE is, no doubt, the pivot of an administration, and no one will deny that the smoothness of the government machinery in His Highness's Dominions at the present time is largely due to Sir George Casson Walker, I.C.S., who held the position of Finance Minister in Hyderabad from 1901 to 1910.

One of the first things undertaken by him was the establishment of an up-to-date mint. No coining had been done for ten years, and the coinage had become seriously depleted in consequence. The experiment proved a complete success, and, although silver was not as cheap then as it is now, the coining profits were very large, the government securing a profit of nearly a crore and a half of rupees on their mint expenditure. Good seasons favoured the nine years that Sir George Casson Walker held office, the departments of land revenue, customs, excise, opium and to some extent forests, brought increased receipts to the government exchequer, new cotton factories were established, the State Railway began to be a paying concern, the Berar Settlement yielded a steady annual revenue, and the net result of Sir George Casson Walker's régime was that, whereas in years immediately preceding the period when he took office the government treasury had not had enough to meet calls of quite an ordinary nature upon it, when he left Hyderabad the income paid into the government treasury was annually in excess of the whole year's expenditure.

In 1911, Sir George Casson Walker was succeeded by Mr. R. I. R. Glancy, I.C.S., who was, at the time of his appointment, First Assistant to the Hon'ble the British Resident. Since then there has been a yearly surplus, and there seems to be every reason to believe that this prosperous state of affairs will continue.

In 1320 Fasli (1910-1911) the surplus yielded amounted to Rs. 1,37,48,681 and in 1321 Fasli (1911-1912) it was Rs. 69,38,073.

In the preface to his Budget Note for 1323 Fasli (1913-1914) the Finance Minister says:—"The annual surplus now averages almost half a crore (of rupees), though many capital works are being financed from revenue. Further, in three years time the Berar famine loan and in eight years time the Two Crore loan will be extinguished. British government rupees eighteen lakhs a year are now devoted to the payment of these two loans. Finally there is every reason to anticipate a steady increase in revenue as the country is developed by roads, railways and irrigation. Of course famine may at any time cause a set back to the prosperity of the State, but people and government are now better prepared to face such a calamity than they were fifteen years ago when the last serious famine occurred."

The government revenue receipts for 1321 Fasli (1911-1912) were Rs. 5,04,13,240, and the principal heads of revenue during that period were as follows :—

	M. S. Rs.
Land Revenue ..	2,34,20,266
Customs	74,42,720
Excise	81,51,635
Opium	7,04,825
Forest	9,11,020
Stamps	9,57,466

	M. S. Rs.
Registration	97,295
Mines	78,276
Berar Rent	29,16,667
Interest	28,54,263
Post Office	4,21,490
Mint	3,42,013

It will be noticed that the revenue derived from excise was very great, and it may be added that this source of revenue is yearly increasing. H. E. the Minister says in the general summary of the administration report for 1320-1321 Fasli (1910-12):—"As a result of the elimination of the Jagir competition and the gradual establishment of complete government control over the excise administration, the excise revenue continues to expand. The revenue derived from the sale of country spirits, sendhi, and mohwa flowers, was in 1321 Fasli Rs. 81,70,538."

It is satisfactory to learn from the same administration report that the duty on liquor is to be increased and an attempt will be made to reduce the consumption of spirits throughout the Dominions "which is at the present time admitted to be excessive."

The government expenditure during 1321 Fasli (1911-1912), was Rs. 4,38,15,094, and the following figures show the different heads of account during that time:—

	M. S. Rs.
Land Revenue ..	37,46,974
Refunds and Compensation	17,51,976
Customs	7,39,262
Excise and Opium ..	1,55,983
Forest	2,32,559
Stamps and Registration ..	1,61,156
Mines	30,478
Interest	8,02,849
Post Office	4,94,387
Mint	4,94,387
General Administration ..	19,01,848
Law and Justice ..	13,95,853
Police	32,99,397
Education	10,19,778
Medical	11,56,079
Minor Departments ..	3,95,387
Contribution to Municipality	5,11,168
Payments to His Highness	50,00,000
Stipends and Allowances ..	45,64,606
Miscellaneous Civil Charges	32,17,802
Settlement of old State Debts	22,63,381
Irrigation and Public Works Department ..	53,37,297

			M. S. Rs.
Military	..	..	53,62,575
Railways	..	..	3,43,921
Adjustments	..	..	2,08,365

The grant for the construction of new roads in 1321 Fasli (1911-1912), was only Rs. 3,37,639, and the Superintending Engineer, in submitting his report for that period, referred to the inadequacy of this grant and drew attention to the fact that whilst the area of His Highness's Dominions is 82,698 sq. miles, there is only one mile of maintained road for every 41 sq. miles of area.

Only one who has travelled in the four divisions of the State can know how very badly roads are needed in the districts. There is nothing direct to show for roads in the way of dividends, but they are really more necessary for the development of the State than the Hingoli railway, for instance; and those who have the true interests of the State at heart will rejoice to hear that, according to the administration report for 1320-1321 Fasli (1910-1912) "a comprehensive programme of road construction has been put in hand."

Local Boards in the districts have since 1887 been in receipt of a cess of one anna per rupee of land revenue, and this money, which is called Local Fund, is partly spent on the repair of roads. But the money thus received is not sufficient for road construction.

When I asked a gentleman who holds a high position in His Highness's government why the roads are so few and so bad in the State, he blamed the Public Works Department, which has the care of them, and said that want of enterprise and not want of money is the cause of the undeveloped state of the Dominions by means of roads to-day.

This may be true, or it may be false, but I know that roads are one of the greatest needs of the State at the present time.

CHAPTER IX.

IRRIGATION.

ANY one who has travelled through Hyderabad State in April and May will realize that irrigation is of supreme importance in the Dominions. Fierce, hot winds tear then across the plains, drying up the water and baking the land. People hide indoors, and animals, with heads hanging down, look in vain for a green leaf or a blade of grass. The coming monsoon is the only topic of conversation, and the blue-grey sky is anxiously scanned for a cloud, if "no bigger than a man's hand." The jowari fields that delight tourists in the cold weather, and have been compared by Americans with the maize prairies of South America, have vanished, and the parched earth fills the sceptic with fears of drought and famine.

In the Telingana water is stored in tanks. In the Marathwara wells are relied upon for water. Famines from time to time occur, and since 1876, government relief works have, during periods of scarcity, been carried on, such as constructing wells and extending and making roads, and those who cannot work have received food and shelter from the government.

The importance of storing water was understood even by the ancient Hindu rulers; but most of the great reservoirs in the State were made by the Kings of Golconda, and the Nizams and their ministers. The Husain Saugar at Hyderabad, which extends, when full, over an area of 8 sq. miles, and supplies water to Hyderabad and Secunderabad, dates from 1575 A.D., when Sultan Ibrahim Kutb Shah built a dam on which, now, the wealth of Hyderabad and the beauty of Secunderabad meet, at sunset. In fact, since the energetic Mint Master lighted the Bund by electricity in September 1913, the road that separates Hyderabad from Secunderabad has become one of the pleasantest places in H. H. the Nizam's Dominions.

The beautiful Mir Alum tank, to the south-west of the city, the Pakhal Lake in the Warangal division, which covers nearly 13 sq. miles, the Afzal Saugar, the Ibrahimpatan, the Jalpalli and other tanks, bear witness to the sagacity and public spirit of rulers who have been and who are no more. And now Hyderabad is to have yet another great tank, and one that will most happily commemorate the accession of H. H. Mir Osman Ali Khan to the throne of his forefathers.

After the terrible flood of 1908, which was the highest and most disastrous that had occurred in Hyderabad for at least three-quarters of a century, and which was caused by the overflow of the river Musi, that generally runs in a small, turgid stream below the city wall, the government of His Highness the late Nizam engaged the services of Mr. M. Visvesvaraya, B.A., C.E., M.INST.C.E., Superintending Engineer, P.W.D., Bombay (now Dewan of Mysore), to advise and assist in the reconstruction of the city and to devise measures for the prevention of the recurrence of such a terrible catastrophe. He was ably assisted by Mr. Ahmed Ali, F.C.H., now secretary to government, P. W. D., Hyderabad, and after much investigation and deliberation these gentlemen gave it as their opinion that the immunity of Hyderabad city from flood must come from the construction of flood catchment areas in the basin above the city, and they proposed to construct two such reservoirs a few miles above the capital, which would be large enough to store all the water ordinarily available for developing irrigation in the valley, and these reservoirs were to cost 56 lakhs of rupees for flood prevention and 45 lakhs for irrigation.

On his accession to the *gadi*, H. H. the present Nizam sanctioned a portion of this scheme, namely, the damming of the river Musi at Gundipett, a project having as its dual object the mitigation of the possible inundation of the city by flood and the supply of pure drinking water to the populations of Hyderabad and Secunderabad.

On March 23rd, 1913, His Highness the Nizam laid the first stone of the Osman Saugar Reservoir, in the presence of the Hon'ble the British Resident, H. E. the Minister, the members of His Highness's government and the leading inhabitants of the city and its suburbs.

An address was read by A. T. Mackenzie, Esq., Superintending Engineer, Irrigation Branch, P. W. D., and he said :—

" Your Highness, Colonel Pinhey, ladies and gentlemen,—The history of this work will not take long to relate. It began in calamity. Let us hope it may end in blessing. None who were here will ever forget the disastrous flood of September 1908. I need not descant upon the loss of life and property, the widespread havoc and suffering it caused. It was the talk of the world. His Highness the late Nizam and his advisers determined then and there that everything humanly possible must be done to prevent such another catastrophe, and in this determination and in the action it called forth none took a greater part than one who has now left Hyderabad but who retains—I have it from his own lips and all who knew him will be certain of it without his declaration—who retains, I say, a deep and loving interest in this State and its inhabitants, for whom he did so much. I refer to Sir George Casson Walker. (Applause.) Without him it is not too much to say that this work would never have come into being and with his name must be coupled that of his successor, Mr. Glancy. (Applause.)

"His late Highness's advisers were fortunate in the officer selected to plan a method of protection. The choice fell upon Mr. Visvesvaraya, one of the ablest of India's engineers, a man who would make his mark in any walk of life, and who is now doing splendid service as Dewan of Mysore. It is to him that we are indebted for the scheme which we are now commencing. The details have been published in the form of a report which all may read and which need not be recapitulated here. In this report he has borne cordial testimony to the great assistance he received from Mr. Ahmed Ali and to the high qualities shewn by that officer in the course of the investigation.

"Mr. Visvesvaraya's scheme has not been materially altered. It has, however, received an addition of great importance. The occasion has been seized not only to protect the city from floods but also to provide it with a pure and bountiful supply of drinking water, the first requisite of health and well-being in any country, but in India above all. We hope that in four years the city of Hyderabad and the cantonment of Secunderabad will be blessed with a supply of water that for purity, copiousness and permanence, can challenge comparison with any town in the East. (Applause.)

"A word may be permitted concerning the magnitude of the work. For this is no light undertaking. In no part of the world would it be a small matter to dam up a river draining nearly 300 sq. miles of country and subject to violent floods, with a wall 125 feet high, to transform it into a placid lake three or four times the area of the Husain Saugar, and capable of containing ten times the quantity of water, to construct a covered conduit twelve miles long, and a pipe system for nearly a million people. There have been big engineering works carried out in India. This in its boldness and width of view is as big as any. It may be confidently asserted that it is by far the biggest thing ever done in Hyderabad. Your Highness will be glad to know that you have in Mr. Dalal an officer eminently capable of bringing this great effort to a successful conclusion, and in this I speak with knowledge, for I have seen and studied and admired the difficult and arduous enterprise of a similar nature that he has already carried out in Mysore.

" It will not be out of place to point out that this work at which we are now assembled is but an instalment. It only half protects Hyderabad from floods, it much reduces their intensity, but it does not confer entire immunity. The river Easi has still to be controlled, an even larger and more costly work, but one which can be applied to a purpose which in India is of overwhelming importance in irrigation. It will not come in my time, but I sincerely hope that His Highness who is young and by God's blessing strong and vigorous, will some day complete the whole scheme which he is now here to inaugurate. (Applause.)

"Mention has been made of the officers to whom this work is chiefly due, but above all Hyderabad must thank the Nizam. It would be presumptuous to make more than a passing reference to the insight and decision of character which prompted him to sanction such an undertaking as one of the first very important actions of his reign. This reservoir is, by permission, Your Highness, to be called by your name. I beg you with this trowel to lay the first stone of the Osman Saugar." (Prolonged applause.)

H. H. the Nizam, speaking in Urdu, then said :—" The Hon'ble Colonel Pinhey, the Prime Minister and those present,—Last Sunday I saw in the papers that His Imperial Majesty the King-Emperor personally laid the foundation stone of a reservoir in his capital, London. For this reason I am very glad that I have also the opportunity of performing a similar function, and to-day I personally lay the foundation stone of the new reservoir of my capital. I am glad to accept the proposal of the Prime Minister and the Chief Engineer that the reservoir, which by the Almighty's favour will shortly be completed, be called hereafter by my name. (Applause.) I considered all the difficulties in carrying out such a great project, and am glad that during my reign the first work started should be one of perpetual and continuing benefit to my subjects. I thank God that he has fulfilled my desire. In the same way I hope the work will be successfully completed and the desire of my well-wishers and citizens will be fulfilled. I would like to state that praise is due to Mr. Visvesvaraya, who is at present Dewan of Mysore, in conjunction with Mr. Ahmed Ali Sahib, the Secretary to Government, P. W. D., who propounded the scheme and drew the attention of my government to its advantages. Besides these, I appreciate the efforts of those officers who brought the scheme to its present state. (Applause.)

I am also confident that the experienced Engineers, Mr. Mackenzie and Mr. Dalal, who have taken the burden of the execution of the work on their shoulders, will complete it satisfactorily, and supply good drinking water to Hyderabad and Secunderabad, and also supply water to cultivators, and thereby my Dominions will be benefited. I thank the Hon'ble Colonel Pinhey and others present for associating themselves with me on this notable occasion in my kingdom. In conclusion, I hereby declare that the building of this Saugar shall commence from to-day."

The stone was then lowered into position by Mr. Mackenzie, and afterwards His Highness tapped it three times with a trowel, saying " I declare this stone well and truly laid." On the stone was the following inscription in Urdu and in English:

" This stone was laid by His Highness the Nizam Nawab Osman Ali Khan Bahadur, G.C.S.I., in the second year of his reign, 1913 A.D."

The Hon'ble Colonel Pinhey called for three cheers for His Highness, and after these had been given, 101 dynamite blasts were fired by electricity on the rocky side of the gorge beyond and great pieces of granite were blown into the air and fell in showers of stone and dust. When the excitement had subsided, His Highness went with the Resident and the Prime Minister to the bed of the river and made himself acquainted with what was being done on the spot; and afterwards he returned with Colonel Pinhey to Hyderabad, leaving the proposed reservoir in the care of the Irrigation Branch of the P. W. D.

CHAPTER X.

THE ADMINISTRATION OF JUSTICE.

THE High Court of the Dominions has since the flood of 1908 been in a building at Saifabad, a suburb of the capital, and the small rooms and narrow passages of this place call loudly for a larger and more imposing-looking building. Plans for a suitable edifice have been prepared, and money is, I believe, available, but so far it has not been found possible to obtain a suitable site.

The present High Court consists of the Chief Justice, five Puisne Judges, and one Mufti, whose decision, according to Mahomedan law, is sent to H. H. the Nizam together with the sentence of the High Court, for all sentences of death and life-long imprisonment.

The High Court has three Benches—the Original Bench, the Divisional Bench and the Full Bench. It maintains a general supervision over all the Courts in the State, and the Chief Justice, or any Judge of the High Court whom he may appoint, goes on circuit from time to time to inspect the various courts in the city and the districts. The High Court issues rules and regulations for the guidance of all the courts, in consonance with the law, alters laws and suggests to the government the introduction of new laws and the amendment of old ones.

There is, also, a Judicial Committee, composed of Judges, which resembles to some extent the Privy Council in England.

In the capital are the Darul Kaza Court, which exercises jurisdiction in original suits between Mahomedans relating to betrothal, marriage, divorce, guardianship, dowry, inheritance, gifts and funeral expenses, and the City Civil and the City Criminal Courts. And in the suburbs of the city are the Atraf-i-balda Court and the Courts of the British Resident.

In each of the four divisions of the State is a Divisional Judge, and the talukdars and tahsildars in the districts have the powers of first, second and third grade magistrates. Even the police patel, or village policeman, has power over low-class people, being able to lock up a prisoner for a few hours or inflict a fine of one or two rupees. The talukdars have, in busy places, Judicial Assistants, and from their courts complicated cases are sent to the Divisional Courts at head-quarters.

The Paigah nobles and the jagirdars have their own courts and prisons, and they possess magisterial powers of various grades which add very much to their importance.

Prisoners from the Atraf-i-balda (crown land) are sent to the Central Jail in Hyderabad. The First Talukdar of the Atraf-i-balda district is a Nazim-i-Diwani, or Civil Judge ; and he has a Judicial Assistant, who presides over the District Civil Court. The second and third tahsildars exercise powers of the third class. The first talukdar is the head of the Atraf-i-balda district police, and he has a superintendent as his executive deputy.

The City Courts are small and very crowded, and the visitor to Hyderabad who desires to witness picturesque and varied scenes should visit the City Criminal Court during the morning hours. Every variety of costume may be seen there and a babel of tongues will be heard, while lawyers and litigants jostle one another on the steep steps, policemen and prisoners arrive and depart, and a varied and motley crowd of onlookers passes up and down. Many lawyers will be noticed, for the legal profession is popular in Hyderabad, and the supply of pleaders is said to exceed the demand. The Hyderabad turban is worn by the lawyers, but no wig or gown.

Law classes and examinations in Urdu, Persian, and Arabic are held in the city, and law students are trained there in civil and criminal law, as it is practised in the various courts in H. H. the Nizam's Dominions, and *sanads* are granted to successful students, which enable them to become pleaders in Hyderabad. These *sanads* must be renewed yearly, unless a considerable sum of money is paid for a perpetual *sanad,* and this arrangement is said to keep a control over the lawyers and to prove more effective than the fear of being "struck off the rolls."

The administration report for 1320-1321 Fasli (1910-1912 A.D.), gives some interesting information concerning policemen and prisons; but it must be remembered that the Paigah estates and the jagirs are not included in these government reports.

The city police are under a kotwal, and consist of 440 officers and 3,072 men. They are smart-looking especially the mounted members of the Force, and on langar day

1913 they were seen to great advantage. The way in which they handled the vast crowds on that occasion was wonderful to witness. But if the handling of masses of people in the streets were equally rough in British India, then we should see in the native newspapers many complaints. The absence of women no doubt accounted for much of the vigorous treatment, and H. H. the Nizam's subjects seemed rather to enjoy being hammered and driven about. The order maintained in the city now, both by day and night, makes it difficult to realize that not so very many years ago it was not considered safe for Europeans to venture there without an escort. And it must not be forgotten that there is no Arms Act in Hyderabad, and that almost every man there carries a weapon of some sort.

The district police are under an Inspector-General, an English gentleman who has devoted the best years of his life to the Hyderabad State and has done much for the Nizam's subjects. The force consists of 1,187 officers and 8,895 men, and is distributed all over the State. During 1320-1321 Fasli (1910-1912 A.D.), 168 murders were investigated by the district police, 328 robberies, 1,409 cases of house trespass or house-breaking, 959 cases of cattle theft and 2,296 cases of ordinary theft.

There are under the care of the Inspector-General 5 Central and 12 District Jails, also a reformatory for boys, and a criminal leper asylum. And a settlement for the tribes that have been declared criminal has lately been opened on a small scale in the Warangal division. In 1320-1321 Fasli (1910-1912 A.D.) the daily average roll of convicts in all the jails was 2,069, and only 3·8 per cent. of the total number of persons admitted (5,524) were literate. Of the prisoners admitted Hindus formed 49·1 per cent. and 19·1 per cent. were Mahomedans. During the two years under consideration, 16 Christians were admitted; and at the Gulbarga Jail I was told that only one Christian had ever been there and that he, during his term of imprisonment, had become a Mahomedan.

There has been a very marked decrease in the number of convicts admitted into the jails of recent years, and this is attributed to the fact that the prisoners are now taught various trades during their incarceration, and consequently return home with a means of earning an honest living. They learn to make tents, carpets, bricks, and other things, and they work in large gardens, thus supplying the jails with vegetables and lessening the expenses of these places. In fact, I am sure that nowhere in India are jails conducted on better principles than in Hyderabad State, and when we consider how illiterate the prisoners are, and the classes from which they come, we cannot fail to see that the results now arrived at are excellent.

During 1320-1321 Fasli (1910-1912 A.D.) forty-three men were sentenced to life-long imprisonment and six were beheaded.

Capital punishment is not inflicted on women. And in civil cases women of the higher classes do not appear in court, but are represented there by a pleader. In the Gulbarga Jail I saw six women who had committed terrible murders, and were suffering life-long imprisonment. The conditions of these female convicts could no doubt have been made better ; but how can an Elizabeth Fry be found in a country where the ladies are strictly purdah ? Only one hundred years ago all the female prisoners in Newgate (London)—300 women and children—were crowded into two wards and two cells, containing a superficial area of about 190 yards, and one old man and his son performed the duties of warders. Without bedding, the women slept on the floor, the boards of which were raised to supply a sort of pillow. In these rooms they lived, cooked, and washed, and history says that the Governor of Newgate entered this portion of the jail with reluctance.

The kitchen arrangements of the jails in Hyderabad State are particularly satisfactory, and the prisoners are well-fed, well-housed, and well-cared-for. Probably of all the government institutions in H. H. the Nizam's Dominions none are so thoroughly satisfactory as the prisons.

CHAPTER XI.

MEDICAL.

THE total population of Hyderabad State being 13,374,676 persons, it is somewhat surprising to find that during the years 1320-1321 Fasli (October 1910-1912 A.D.) the yearly average of patients treated in the government hospitals and dispensaries was only 767,222 men, women and children, and that the in-patients averaged during the same period only 5,850 persons. The administration report says of the period under consideration :—" While there has been some increase in the number of in-patients, there has been a considerable and continuous decrease in the number of out-patients."

Yet the Census for 1911 shows an extraordinary increase in the total for infirmities in the State since 1901, and says " a 20 per cent. increase of population (from 1901 to 1911) cannot be held to account sufficiently for an one thousand per cent. increase in the number of persons suffering from the infirmities included in the Census."

Possibly plague had something to do with this. The year 1321 Fasli (1912 A.D.) was the most disastrous since plague first entered the Dominions, and in that year the City was for the first time attacked by the epidemic. The total number of plague cases in 1912 was no less than 30,632 and the deaths numbered 27,367. The masterly manner in which the epidemic was handled and finally stamped out reflects on His Highness's government and on Lieutenant-Colonel H. E. Drake-Brockman, I.M.S., Director of the Medical Department, vast credit; but the evil effects of the scourge may possibly have had something to do with the great increase in the number of persons suffering from the four infirmities mentioned in the Census, and more especially with the fact that no less than 16,263 persons are returned in it as blind, while in the Census of 1901 only 1,344 persons were returned as suffering from that infliction. The Census for 1911 says that blindness claims sixty per cent. of the total afflicted in the State, and the number of women sufferers equals, and in some places exceeds, that of the men, and it suggests that smoky wood fuel in ill-ventilated kitchens has much to do with the loss of eyesight among the women.

The same authority states that the Mahomedans are better off than the Hindus in respect of all infirmities except insanity; and that the Animists, who live a simple life, free from the worries of rains and crops, sowcars and sircars, are better off as regards infirmities than either Hindus or Mahomedans.

The Census for 1911 gives the following figures for the four principal infirmities of the State—insane 2,560, deaf-mute 4,421, leper 3,785, blind 16,263, and it says that the worst period as regards these afflictions is for the men from 40 to 45 and for the women from 60 to 65. The largest proportion of lepers occurs at the age period 40-45. Far fewer females than males become lepers, but the Census thinks that women can more easily hide this infirmity than is the case with men.

There are in the State 91 government hospitals and dispensaries, and the Afzalganj and Victoria hospitals in Hyderabad city are the only government hospitals of any size or importance. The former has an average of 62,120 in and out-patients per annum; and the latter, which is strictly purdah, treated during 1912 10,808 out-patients and 1,516 in-patients—chiefly maternity cases.

I will now briefly describe my visit to the Afzalganj hospital in October 1913, because by doing so I can give the best idea of what this hospital needs at the present time.

I had received an introduction to a minor official, and on my arrival, at about 11 A.M., he called a peon and sent me to the room of the head surgeon. This place was empty, but an open door led into an operating chamber, and I was told that I could go in there, if I liked. The screams proceeding from the operating theatre were so agonising that I left the surgeon's room in a hurry and returned to the person to whom I had an introduction, and after considerable hesitation and much explanation he promised to show me the hospital after the doctors had gone away. So I waited until the doctor Sahibs had finished their business, watching the windows of the operating theatre, outside which stood crowds of men with heads thrust forward and eyes fixed, no doubt, on the patient, and thinking of the time when, in England, lunatics, prisoners and sick persons had been sights that the public delighted to visit. That was not so very long ago, and but for Florence Nightingale might still be the same, perhaps. Now, in England, kings and queens visit hospitals and send gifts of game, fruit, and other things to the patients, rich people endow beds in and leave large sums of money to hospitals, and well-educated and refined women nurse the sick and attend to the dying. And in British India, the wives of viceroys and governors all try to follow the royal example as regards hospitals and nurses.

Government charity must always be a cold and barren business; yet in a purdah country how can any woman become a Florence Nightingale and make hospital nursing fashionable? The care of the sick and suffering is, no doubt, woman's special province, and what women can do in Hyderabad in this direction is proved by the Victoria Zenana Hospital, which was visited in September 1913 by the late Lady Hardinge. and pronounced by her to be up-to-date and excellent. But in a hospital where men are nursed, as well as women and children, no purdah lady can set foot, and probably that is the real reason why government mixed hospitals and dispensaries are so unpopular all over His Highness the Nizam's Dominions.

It was 12 A.M. before I could go over the Afzalganj Hospital, and then the drains seemed to overflow with disinfectants. Dressings were being carried away, and a foul smell met me at every turn in the over-crowded wards, and the whole place depressed me past words, although the minor official assured me that in his time great improvements had been made and that he remembered the day when men and women wore the same uniform and messed together on the open verandahs. The under-paid and over-worked nurses, the dirty blankets, the herding of children with grown-up people—well it all cried loudly for Florence Nightingale, the woman of whom Queen Victoria wrote, "She has such a clear brain. I wish we had her at the War Office."

The total expenditure by government on the Medical Department in 1321, Fasli (1912 A.D.), was 6,35,520 O. S. rupees; and it may be noticed that expenditure on this department has of late years become less and less and that during 1320-1321 Fasli (1910-1912 A.D.), not one rupee was spent on buildings.

In the districts I visited many hospitals and dispensaries, and I found them clean, but badly equipped and wanting in medicines and instruments. Many reasons were assigned for this state of affairs, and a missionary doctor, who has an up-to-date hospital and a good private practice, assured me that the government would supply the necessary medicines and other things if the people in charge of the hospitals and dispensaries did not take them home and sell them! I was "minded" to ask the Director of the Medical Department about these matters; and one day, when I happened to be at a small railway station in the Medak district, I very nearly did so, for one of the carriages of an in-coming train was labelled "Reserved for Lieutenant-Colonel Drake-Brockman." But it was only about 9 A.M., and I was told that the doctor Sahib was asleep, and I felt sure that if I woke him up, he would not give me the information I needed, for officials belonging to H. H. the Nizam's service will seldom answer any question that is put to them. Polite they are, but very discreet, and the enquirer is sent from office to office until he learns to "read, mark, learn, and inwardly digest" official documents.

A government medical school in the capital trains both sexes to become doctors and surgeons, and during 1320-1312 Fasli (1910-1912 A.D.), fourteen students passed out of it, five as Assistant Surgeons, and nine as Sub-Assistant Surgeons.

The Yunani (native treatment) branch of the Medical Department has its own medical school, and it is said that the training given there includes Misri (Egyptian) treatment. The Yunani dispensaries in the districts have increased of late, but no statistics as to the number of people treated in these places are available. Such dispensaries are in the districts largely supported by local funds, and receive a little help from the government.

The Lunatic Asylum is in the Hyderabad Central Jail, and during 1320-1321 Fasli (1910-1912 A.D.), 284 lunatics were there; and it is said that about 38·3 per cent. of the cases of insanity in the State are caused by an excessive use of narcotics.

Of the sanitary department, organised since 1912, no report has as yet been published by His Highness's government.

CHAPTER XII.

EDUCATION.

THE education problem occupies a large place in the minds of His Highness's government to-day, and no stone is being left unturned that is likely to hide under it the secret of the illiteracy of the masses in the Nizam's Dominions.

Says the new Census :—"The proportion of literates per one thousand persons in Hyderabad State is 28, which compares very unfavourably with the figures for the Central Provinces and Behar, and the Bombay and Madras Presidencies, and the Baroda and Mysore States.

Hyderabad	28
Bombay	70
Madras	75
Baroda	101
Mysore	63
Central Provinces and Behar	33

Not long ago His Highness's government engaged the services of an English educational expert from British India, and after spending two years in studying the problem of education in Hyderabad State, this gentleman published a long report that does not seem to have given much satisfaction. Now a learned and academic Mahomedan gentleman is in charge of the Education Department, and of him it was said to me by a gentleman from Bombay, to whom he had offered a post in the Hyderabad educational service, "His ideas are alarmingly magnificent."

I do not suppose that my opinion can be of much value, but I will say that while travelling in the districts, it seemed to me that in a country like Hyderabad, where roads are so badly needed and where, in consequence, the people do not mix freely or have much intellectual stimulus, education must be made popular among the Hindus before it can become general. I do not think that the figures given in administration reports include missionary schools, in fact, a missionary who is in charge of large schools for boys and girls told me, "We avoid the Education Department as much as possible," but missionaries have assured me that the Hindu children whom they teach seldom show much intelligence. There is, in fact, little to rouse the intelligence of Hindu children in places far from a railway station and reached only by a fair-weather road or a cart-track, and it seems to me that if the Hindu religion were not so much neglected in government schools, there might be a desire on the part of parents to let their children learn the things that the Education Department is so anxious to teach them, for with Hindus religion is not only a duty but, also, a stimulus.

As it is now, parents in the districts want to make money by their children as soon as the boys and girls can earn a few annas, and they prefer to send their sons to the so-called "bazaar schools," where pupils come and go as their parents please, no regular hours are insisted upon and, above all, there are no examinations. Government schools are too strict as regards clothes and cleanliness to suit illiterate parents, and they prefer to pay a few dubs to a Hindu schoolmaster, who in some small, ill-ventilated room will teach the boys to repeat by heart some well-known Hindu legends, and to do a little bazaar arithmetic.

There is no gainsaying that while the government is most anxious to educate the masses, employers, in country places, are just as desirous to keep them in slavish ignorance. The sowcars, too, hinder education all they can. Said to me a sowcar: "If a Hindu speaks English, I have no use for him."

And then it is just possible that the language of the ruling community is made too prominent in government schools, and that Telegu, Marathi, and Canarese do not receive sufficient attention, for we find that the percentage of Mahomedan boys who go to government schools is much higher than that of Hindus. The following figures were given to me by the Education Department for 1322 Fasli (1913 A.D.); and it must be remembered that there are in the State 11,620,146 Hindus and only 1,380,990 Mahomedans.

Total number of pupils attending government schools of all grades, and percentage:

Mahomedans ..	28,715	percentage	41·2
Hindus ..	37,143	,,	53·3
Christians ..	2,706	,,	4·0
Parsis ..	119	,,	0·1
Others ..	991	,,	1·4

The Census says: "There were in 1901 in the elementary schools 80,743 scholars, and in 1911 there were only 76,065. The youngest generation is being practically kept away from schools to a far larger extent than was the case ten years ago." And it contrasts the present with the previous Census as follows :—

1901.

Population under 10	..	2,808,521
Literate under 10	..	14,937

1911.

Population under 10	..	3,618,680
Literate under 10	..	9,493

Secondary education has, however, during the last decade made conspicuous progress, and while in 1901 the number of scholars attending secondary schools was 13,826, the number had risen in 1911 to 16,326. Higher education is provided for by the following institutions :

The Nizam's College, which has an English Principal, and is affiliated to the Madras University. To this College a Madrassa-i-Aliya or School department is attached, also hostels for the accommodation of students who come to the capital from a distance.

The Dar-ul-uloom or Oriental College, in Hyderabad city, where students study

Islamic theology, law and literature and are trained to become Moulvis and Munshis.

Twenty-one High Schools, 9 Vernacular, 7 English under government management, and 5 English under aided agency.

Fifty-eight Middle Schools, 31 managed by government, 4 by the Sarf-i-khas department, 17 by aided, and 6 by unaided agencies.

By giving scholarships and in other ways the Hyderabad government does its utmost to encourage learning and to assist students of both sexes, but the results are not very encouraging at the present time.

Says the Census :—"The statistics of University examinations show a considerable falling off in the number of candidates, who matriculated in the year 1911. Out of 26 candidates only 2 passed, the corresponding figures for 1901 being 112 and 18 respectively. This large decrease in the number of students entering the University course of study is but the reflex of the general retrogression in the lowest stages during the decade. There is no change in the figures relating to the Intermediate examination. The number of candidates for the B.A. examination also showed a considerable decline. Altogether higher education must be said to be languishing."

A Civil Service class has lately been opened again at the Nizam College, and of this, the Finance Minister said in the preface to his Budget Note for 1323 Fasli (1913-1914): "If there were no other reforms of any kind to record this year, the institution of a regular Civil Service would render the year remarkable. The first batch of students has now been selected after examination, they will go through a course of two years' training at the Nizam College and of one year's practical training in British India."

It may also be mentioned that a technical class in connection with the government workshops at the Mint has been opened, on a small scale, and that it is hoped to provide thus, later on, technical education of a serviceable type.

Having seen that the attendance at school is much higher among Mahomedans than Hindus, it is not surprising to read in the Census that per 1,000 inhabitants, 59 Mahomedans, and 23 Hindus are literate. And we read that of the Animists, who number 285,722 of His Highness's subjects, only 247 are literate. The figures given in the Census are said not to be very accurate as concerns the jagirs; but they go to prove that the jagirdars (taken *en masse*) are not anxious to see their ryots advance in education, and that they do little in the way of jagir schools.

The Census speaks of "the almost total illiteracy of the female population," but notices that the Mahomedans have a much larger proportion of women (as of men) literates than the Hindus. No mention is made of the zenana schools in the capital, which are said to be as good, if not better, than similar schools in British India. The Madrassa-i-Aizza Niswania School for the daughters of the official middle class, has been in existence for more than a quarter of a century, and in this institution over one hundred Mahomedan girls are prepared for the Hyderabad Middle School, and the Madras University Matriculation examinations. The education given in this school includes geometry, algebra, physiology, physics and chemistry, also Urdu, Persian, English and enough Arabic for religious purposes.

In the Mamhubia Girls' School, which was opened a few years ago for the daughters of the Hyderabad aristocracy, an elaborate attempt is made to cultivate the minds of the pupils and prepare them for the lives they will lead when married. And here the Indian and English ladies of Hyderabad meet once a month for recreation and improvement.

The non-purdah Methodist High School for the daughters of the lower middle classes is quite up-to-date, and has a large attendance.

In 1321 Fasli (1911 A.D.), the average number of girls under instruction in all the schools in the State was 6,017—2,907 Mahomedans, 1,962 Hindus, 1,068 Christians, and 45 Parsis.

I venture to disagree with a member of His Highness's government in his opinion that the illiteracy of the masses in Hyderabad State is largely due to the fact that the girls of the lower classes are kept totally ignorant. It seems to me that the whole environment of the people in the districts is at fault, and that a desire for more education will come when roads open up the districts, the jagirdars are brought to a sense of their great responsibilities as landlords, and some Hindu religious text-book is introduced into the primary schools. It is not, it seems to me, the educational system that needs to be improved, but what the Hindu pupils want in the primary schools is less red tape and more encouragement.

CHAPTER XIII.

THE SINGARENI COLLIERIES.

COAL mining being one of the most important industries in Hyderabad State, I was anxious to visit the Singareni collieries at Yellandu, and journeyed to Dornakal Junction, which has become quite a busy place since the adjacent coalfields brought it into prominence. There was no available train from Dornakal to Yellandu before midnight, and then, after an hour's journey, I reached a dark little station, where I was advised to sleep in the railway carriage until daybreak. The jabber of coolies woke me before the sun was up, and the servant said that these people had been waiting on the platform all night in the hope of carrying my traps to the Rest House, and that I must walk there, because Yellandu possesses no public conveyance of any sort. The distance was not great, and, followed by a crowd of men and women, who fought for my things and seemed to talk a dozen languages, I reached in a few minutes the best Rest House

I have found in Hyderabad State, in fact, it was so good, I began to fear that I had come by mistake into one of the luxurious places that His Highness's State Railway reserves so jealously for the use of its officers and their friends.

Singareni, as seen from the Rest House, did not resemble any mining centre I had visited in other parts of the world, and apart from a small line along which ran empty trucks, there was nothing to intimate that I was on a coalfield. Men, women and boys, carrying lamps, passed in batches and I was told that they were the "miners;" and, later on, Englishmen drove by in neat buggies, and they were pointed out to me as "the mine Sahibs on their way to office." Wood, my servant said, was expensive in the bazaar, but otherwise prices there were the same as in Secunderabad, and he had found an English Memsahib who sold fruits and vegetables, and from her he had obtained big tomatoes and enormous carrots and turnips. I learnt, later on, that water is only too plentiful in the mines, and, in consequence, everyone in Singareni can have a garden all the year round. Moreover the Company has made a tank, that is developing into a pretty lake, and there fishing, swimming, and a little boating can be indulged in by the mine Sahibs and their Memsahibs. And there is a Club where these people meet twice a week for tennis, billiards, and bridge, and where they give an occasional ball to which all the Europeans for many miles round are invited. The Company has built a church, and, when I was there, Singareni had just escaped having a Bishop, the Bishop of Madras having been anxious to make a See at Singareni for Bishop Azariah, and to convert the Company's pretty little church into a cathedral of some sort.

At sunset I went to the office, where the English manager gave me a bundle of papers in which I could find the information I wanted, and he promised that one of his English staff should call for me early the following morning and drive me round the twenty pits, which stretch over a considerable distance.

I read that the Singareni coalfields were discovered in 1872 by Dr. King of the Indian Geological Survey Department, and in 1886 the Hyderabad-Deccan Company acquired the mining rights from His Highness's government. English miners were afterwards sent to lay out the works of an English colliery, and since that time the coalfields have expanded, although, perhaps, the coal industry has not become all that was hoped and expected of it twenty years ago. Four distinct seams have now been found, the principal one being the King seam, which contains a valuable, hard, semi-bituminous steam coal, and which is being worked at a considerable depth, some of the works being not less than 1,400 feet from the surface.

The main shaft is at the Osman pit (named after H. H. the Nizam when he was a little boy), and this accommodates the King seam. Here the tubs of coal are brought to the bottom of the shaft on rails, run by a cable that is worked by electric power, and the tubs, which contain eleven hundredweight of coal each, are raised to the pit's surface in cages, two at a time, and the coal is then tipped on to an endless revolving belt, from which women and boys extract the shale and outside products before it travels to the end of the belt, and there falls into wagons that convey it to the railway station.

All this I saw the next morning, but I did not go down the shaft, being satisfied with recollections of mines I had explored elsewhere. I saw the miners—men, women and boys—going down, sixteen at a time, and I noticed that they laughed and talked and did not seem to be at all nervous. Some years ago it was different. Then miners had to be brought to Singareni from the north of India. But now a miner's life is popular at Yellandu, good wages, good houses and good compensation in case of death, or accident, having convinced the people in the neighbourhood that a miner's work is worth the risks that must attend on mining. Stalwart men from the neighbourhood of Lucknow still help to hew the coal, but the ordinary work is done by the people of Yellandu.

The coal is won by contract, the headman of each gang being paid monthly according to the number of yards cut. And the work, which is in eight hours' shifts, goes on both night and day, except during the many Hindu holidays, Christmas Day, and the Mohurrum. Englishmen superintend the work underground, and they possess the confidence of the Indian miners, who say: "If there is an accident, the English Sahibs never leave us." The neat houses of the miners and their well-stocked gardens were pleasant to visit, the bazaar was clean, and the Company's hospital looked well-cared-for and up-to-date.

The machinery used in the mines is of the best and latest pattern; the electrical power station gives just under 1,000 h.p.; and the water is pumped out of the mines by a treble ram pipe, which discharges 600 gallons of water per minute at the surface, from a depth of nearly 800 feet.

There are 8,315 persons working in the mines—6,406 below and 1,909 above, and during the two past years 38 fatal accidents have occurred.

During the years 1910, 1911 and 1912 there has been unfortunately a constant decrease in the output of the coalfields, and consequently of the royalty paid to His Highness's government. The administration report for 1320-1321 Fasli (1910-1912 A.D.), gives the following figures:—

1910	Output	506,173 tons	Royalty paid	56,914	O. S. rupees.
1911	,,	505,380 ,,	,,	56,855	,,
1912	,,	481,652 ,,	,,	51,186	,,

CHAPTER XIV.

THE COTTON INDUSTRY.

COTTON being the largest export of Hyderabad State, the cotton industry holds an important place in the eyes of His Highness's government.

The area of cultivated land under cotton to-day is three million acres, and most of the cotton is grown in the Maratha districts, where the soil is peculiarly well-suited to it.

The opening of the Hyderabad-Godavari Railway, in October 1900, gave a great impetus to the growth of cotton in the Nizamabad, Nander, Parbhani and Aurangabad Districts, where many ginning and pressing factories came into existence as soon as heavy machinery could be brought there by rail. Bombay buyers then began to arrive in considerable numbers during the cotton season, which lasts from October to December, and as they paid cash for the cotton and would even send coolies to cut it and bring it to the cotton marts, more and more land began to be put down in cotton by the ryots. Hand-gins gave place to ginning machines, and the ryots ceased to weed their fields carefully, and to cultivate only the best cotton. Grain and pulses then became more expensive, so much of the best land being laid down in cotton, and Marathwara entered upon a critical period of its existence. Says the new Census :—" The evolution from the agricultural to the manufacturing stage has already begun in Marathwara.......When a country begins to produce the raw materials of manufacture in place of food crops, it has started on the road to industrialisation."

One of the most serious developments, after the ginning and pressing factories sprang up, was the mixing of the three sorts of cotton grown in the State—the Gaorani, Nambhri, and Bharat varieties.

In the days of hand-gins, Gaorani, which is said to be the indigenous variety, had by its long staple gained for Hyderabad cotton a high place in the cotton marts. But the buyers, who came in numbers from Bombay and elsewhere, showed a preference for Bharat, which has a short staple, but is a hardy coarse cotton that will stand rough handling and climatic difficulties, and yields a far larger crop per acre than the Gaorani variety.

And, to make matters worse, some buyers mixed the three varieties together and sold the mixture as "pure Gaorani," thus causing in the spinning rooms "weeping and gnashing of teeth."

During the last four or five years Hyderabad cotton has been losing its good name in the cotton markets, and although exports have not fallen off, the prices paid locally have become less and less. So in November 1912, the Director of the new Department of Agriculture went to investigate "the rapid deterioration in progress in the fields around the chief cotton marts," and he came to the conclusion that Bharat is preferred by the buyers because it can be soaked. Water adds weight, and Bharat does not show water, while Gaorani becomes yellow when it is damped.

No one denies that at Parbhani, and the other cotton centres, the cotton is watered in ginning and pressing factories once, twice and even three times, before being pressed; but then the same thing is done in other parts of India, and the cotton *looks* none the worse for it. The Director suggested a Cotton Adulteration Act, and if it be true that Bharat has ousted Gaorani because the latter cannot be watered, then, no doubt, such an Act might prove very beneficial. But his former chief, the Director-General, Revenue Department, wrote that "many years ago, there existed the Bombay Cotton Frauds Act, but it was found unworkable, and after a few years' experience was repealed."

"No legislation," said this gentleman, "can prevent a practice of this kind, carried on, as it is, openly, with the knowledge of purchasers and consumers."

I believe I am right in saying that, about three years ago, watering cotton in ginning and pressing factories in Berar was stopped by order of government, and that this order has benefited all persons except the buyers, who desire to add weight to their bales of cotton by means of water.

Mixing cannot be stopped by order of government, but watering can, and that without much trouble.

The remedy proposed by the former Director-General, Revenue Department, was "to pursue a steady course of selecting good seed, and proving to the ryots and the trade that unadulterated Gaorani cotton is the most profitable both to the producer and the consumer." And this he said was to be done by planting Gaorani cotton on government farms. "The policy of the Agricultural Department," he said, "is not to establish large expensive model farms, but rather to demonstrate by small experiments in various parts of the country, what can be done at a reasonable cost."

"If a thing is worth doing at all, it is worth doing well," and when I visited these government farms in 1913, I found them much too small to do more than look well on paper. As to Gaorani seed, the ryots can get it from the men who still buy nothing but Gaorani cotton; but they prefer to buy mixed seed because the present demand is for mixed cotton—that is to say for Bharat, with a little Gaorani and a little Nambhri mixed with it.

I have read in one of Maharaja Sir Kishen Pershad's administration reports that provision has been made in the administration for special commissions, and I think that much good might be done if such a commission were to enquire into the management of the ginning and pressing factories, the injury done to cotton seed by the machinery used to-day, the mixing of the three varieties of cotton and the excessive damping of the same before the cotton is pressed, the cotton seed that is now exported to Europe, the 50 per cent. interest taken by sowcars in the cotton districts, and many kindred subjects.

There are in the State three large spinning and weaving mills and about 90 small ginning and pressing factories. The population supported by cotton spinning, sizing, and weaving is 69,943 persons; and by cotton ginning, cleaning, and pressing, 517,750 men, women, and children. The wages paid to the employés in these places are good, but the cost of living in Marathwara is very high, owing to the many holdings that are put down in cotton, and the uncertainty of the rainfall, and nowhere are the people more at the mercy of the money-lender than in the cotton country.

The Agricultural Department has opened some small State banks, and these, too, might form a part of the work of the special commission, for the principles on which they have been based are open to comment.

CHAPTER XV.

The Hon'ble the British Resident.

When we visit the Residency bazaars in Hyderabad to-day, and learn that the British Resident now exercises there civil and criminal jurisdiction over 17,971 people, we find it difficult to picture the Residency area of one hundred years ago. At that time the Resident lived in one of the garden houses of the minister of the day and he had little responsibility and little influence.

In "The Nizam," by Henry George Briggs, we find the following curious account of the present fine-looking Residency. Writing to Lady Clive, in October 1799, while passing through Hyderabad on his way to Persia, *via* Bombay, Sir John Malcolm says :—

"I will conclude this letter by relating an anecdote connected with the projected edifice (the Residency) that will satisfy you. The princes of the East do not lose much of their valuable time in the study of geography. Major Achilles Kirkpatrick, the Resident at this Court, wished to obtain a grant of one or two fields to erect this structure upon. He requested the engineer of the English force stationed at Hyderabad to make an exact survey of the spot and when this was finished upon a large sheet he carried it to the Darbar and, showing it to the Nizam, requested he would grant the English Government a grant of the land. The Prince, after gravely examining the survey, said he was sorry he could not comply with the request. When the Resident was retiring, not a little disconcerted at the refusal of a favour which he deemed so trifling, Mir Alum (the minister), said to him, with a smile, "Do not be annoyed. You frightened the Nizam with the size of the plan you showed him. Your fields were almost as large as any of the maps of his kingdom he has yet seen. No wonder," added the Mir, laughing, "he did not like to make such a cession. Make a survey on a reduced scale and the difficulty will vanish." The Resident could hardly believe that this would be the case; but when at his next interview he presented the plan upon a small card, the cheerful assent of the Prince satisfied him that the Mir had been quite correct in his guess at the cause of his former failure." In due course the building was proceeded with, and the Residency was completed in 1807 by Lieutenant S. Russell, of the Madras Engineers.

The attack made on the Residency in 1857 is also very graphically described by Mr. Briggs in his book, "The Nizam."

The growth of the power of the Resident and the importance of the area that now goes by the name of "the Residency Bazaars" was largely due to the fact that the Hon'ble the Resident had to administer the Assigned districts. And the many bankers who now live in the Residency bazaars are said to have been drawn to the neighbourhood by Residents who experienced much difficulty in obtaining good money with which to pay the troops, when there were in the State many mints and many kinds of coins.

The Secunderabad cantonment (six miles north-east of Hyderabad city), where the Resident hoists the British flag during the rains, has now a population of 113,499 persons, including 7,000 English and Indian troops, which form the Secunderabad portion of the 9th Division of the Southern Army, whose headquarters are at Ootacamund. This military station, which is one of the largest in India, was originally the station of the Subsidiary Force. The combined cantonment now comprises Secunderabad, Chikalguda, Bowanpalli, Begampett, Trimulgherry and Bolarum, and covers an area of nineteen square miles.

RESIDENTS AND ACTING RESIDENTS.

Mr. John Holland was the first representative of the Governor-General at the Court of the Nizam, and he arrived at Hyderabad in 1779. He was succeeded by Mr. J. Grant, who retired in 1784.

Mr. R. Johnson	1784
Captain Kennaway	1788
Captain J. A. Kirkpatrick ..	1797
Captain W. A. Kirkpatrick ..	1798
Mr. H. Russell	1805
Captain T. Sydenham	1806
Lieutenant C. Russell	1810
Mr. H. Russell	1811
Mr. C. T. Metcalfe	1820
Captain H. S. Barnett	1825
Mr. W. B. Martin	1825
Mr. E. C. Ravenshaw	1830
Colonel J. Stewart	1830
Major J. Cameron	1838
Brigadier J. Wahab, C.B. ..	1838
Major G. Tomkyns	1838
Colonel J. S. Fraser	1838

Major C. Davidson	1852
Colonel Low, C.B.	1853
Major C. Davidson	1853
Mr. G. A. Bushby	1853
Captain A. R. Thornhill ..	1856
Colonel C. Davidson	1857
Major A. R. Thornhill	1862
Sir J. U. Yule, K.C.S.I., C.B. ..	1863
Sir R. Temple, K.C.S.I.	1867
Mr. G. J. Cordery	1868
Hon'ble A. A. Roberts, C.B., C.S.I. ..	1868
Mr. C. B. Saunders, C.B. ..	1868
Colonel E. C. Ross, C.S.I. ..	1886
Mr. G. J. Cordery	1886
Major D. Robertson	1887
Mr. A. P. Howell	1888
Sir D. Fitzpatrick, K.C.S.I. ..	1889
Mr. T. W. Chichele Plowden, C.S.I., I.C.S.	1891
Hon'ble Lieutenant-Colonel Sir D. W. K. Barr, K.C.S.I.	1901
Hon'ble C. S. Bayley, C.S.I., I.C.S. ..	1905
Hon'ble M. F. O'Dwyer, I.C.S. ..	1908
Hon'ble C. S. Bayley, C.S.I., I.C.S. ..	1908
Lieutenant-Colonel A. F. Pinhey, C.S.I., C.I.E.	1911
Hon'ble S. M. Fraser	1914
Lieutenant-Colonel A. F. Pinhey, C.S.I., C.I.E.	1914

CHAPTER XVI.

THE STATE ARMY.

THE army of H. H. the Nizam, which is by far the largest army of any native ruler in India, consists of irregular troops, regular troops, the Golconda Brigade, the Imperial Service troops, the Nizam Mahbub regiment, and volunteers.

The Irregular Forces, which have to-day an average strength of 13,533, date back to the time of Asaf Jah, and their ancestors were the Arabs, Rohillas, Afghans, Sikhs, Rahtores, Rajputs, and Baluchis who helped the first Nizam to conquer and settle Hyderabad. H. E. the Minister says of them in the administration report for 1320-21 Fasli (October 1910-12) :—" The reduction in the number of irregular troops goes on slowly. Vested interests have to be respected, but the cost of these irregulars, twenty-three and a quarter lakhs a year, is still a very heavy burden to the State."

These irregulars I saw in all their glory on Langar day, 1913; and, in many cases, they seemed to know little of drill and discipline, to wear their own clothes or old-world uniforms, and to carry antique weapons. Some were old, others were boys, and I was told that these picturesque soldiers guard the palaces of His Highness and the great nobles of Hyderabad, furnish escorts, and in the districts, protect the treasuries, escort the mails, and help to discover and arrest dacoits.

The Regular Forces date from 1858 A.D. When the attack was made on the British Residency in Hyderabad, in 1857, most of the Contingent troops had gone to British India to fight there against the mutineers; and afterwards Sir Salar Jung I thought that in an armed State like Hyderabad there ought to be a State army on which H. H. the Nizam could depend in case of internal insurrection and rebellion. So in 1858 he gave power to the Raja of Wonpurty to organise a small army, with guns, which was to be called "the Nizam's Field Force." To this little army more men and more guns were added, also Nawab Nizam Yar Jung's Cavalry; and in 1868 the Nizam's Field

Force developed into the Nizam's Regular Forces, with Major Rooke as Commandant.

The Nizam's Regular Forces, which have to-day an average strength of 46 officers and 3,053 men, are well-armed and well-disciplined, and would, no doubt, if called upon to take the field, do the State great credit. They are composed chiefly of Deccan Mahomedans, other Mahomedans, Rajputs, Maharatas, and Brahmins. The African Cavalry Guards, which now form the bodyguard of His Highness, are all Africans, and it is found very difficult to keep up the strength of this regiment, which began in 1858 with some African slave boys, who were trained and mounted by the Raja of Wonpurty.

The Imperial Service troops comprise 8 officers and 688 men ; and it must not be forgotten that these troops, which now take a prominent place in every native State in India of size and importance, are the direct outcome of the 60 lakhs of rupees offered by H. H. the late Nizam to the British Government, in 1886, for the defence of the Frontier. His example was followed by other Indian princes, and the Government of India then decided that the Indian ruling chiefs should be allowed to raise properly trained and equipped forces to fight side by side with the British regiments in case of need.*

The total cost of the Military Establishment was in 1321 Fasli (1912 A.D.), Rs. 52,34,272 ; and almost half of this money went to pay for the irregular troops, which are now out-of-date and almost useless.

The Regular Forces have several regimental bands, and the most important of them—H. H. the Nizam's band—is composed of string as well as wind instruments, and is conducted by an experienced bandmaster.

The hospitals and dispensaries for the troops I did not see, but I was told that an up-to-date military hospital "has been promised."

The pay of the troops varies from eight to fifteen rupees a month for the Regular Forces and the Imperial Service. Troops can add three rupees a month to their pay by good conduct. Most of the troops are stationed in or near the capital, but some are in the chief towns in the districts. The

* Since this was written the army of H. H. the Nizam has been largely drawn upon for the Expeditionary Forces sent from India to the seat of war in 1914. We may feel sure that the Hyderabad troops will make history in Europe and return home covered with honour and glory, or fall like heroes on the battlefield.

State Army appears to be fairly popular as a means of earning a living, and there is no dearth of officers. These privileged gentlemen have a fine club on the Fateh Maidan, a suburb of Hyderabad city, and they enjoy sports and races at the local gymkhana, in fact, they have a very good time, if one may judge by their appearance.

CHAPTER XVII.

THE MINT.

THE State Mint was moved in 1904 from Hyderabad city to the suburb of Saifabad, and since that time it had seen many important developments.

In 1853, when Sir Salar Jung I began his currency reforms, there was practically no State money. No less than 26 mints coined money at that time, and three rupees—the Bagh Chalni, the Shahr Chalni, and the Hukm Chalni—were then in circulation and each had a different weight and different value. At that time no less than fifty varieties of silver coins were used in the State, to say nothing of copper coins.

The standard of silver currency introduced by the Delhi rulers was nine of silver and two of alloy, and the name of the King of Delhi was on Hyderabad coins until 1858 (the year after the Mutiny). But the standard was much debased in the private mints, and as the rupees were all hand-made, they could be easily manufactured in the city bazaars.

The British Residents constantly protested against the debasement of the currency, which caused the greatest inconvenience to them in obtaining reliable rupees for the payment of the troops and for the monetary transactions of the Residency, and they made constant but unsuccessful attempts to persuade the Nizam to close the private mints in the State and make the East India Company's rupee the sole legal currency. In 1851 Captain Meadows Taylor wrote, "The wretched system of coinage in the Nizam's country, and the indisputable necessity of placing the department on a better footing have been strongly urged by me on Siraj-ul-Mulk, who has promised to give such immediate attention to the subject as its importance deserves."

In 1855 Sir Salar Jung I established a State Bank in Hyderabad city and introduced a silver currency called the Halli Sicca rupee, and this currency, like that of the Delhi rulers, contained nine of silver and two of alloy. The progress of the Halli Sicca rupee was slow, but in 1863 Sir Salar Jung said that the new system of coinage had answered "fairly well," and in 1868 the Government of India adopted the Halli Sicca as the rupee for Hyderabad and fixed the official rate of exchange between it and the British Government rupee at Rs. 16-14-6.

In 1894 a rupee with a milled edge was manufactured by machinery and at that time the Char Minar pattern of rupee was introduced, and with this pattern the present currency of the State is minted.

In 1905, Sir George Casson Walker moved the State Mint to Saifabad, and brought out from England up-to-date machinery for it, some of which has lately been used to open up an Electricity Department. Ever since 1905, silver and copper coins have been minted, and the silver and copper coinage for 1321 Fasli (1911-1912 A.D.) was as follows :—

Rupees	72,39,461
Eight anna silver coins ..	2
Four anna ,, ,, ..	2
Two anna ,, ,, ..	2
Half anna copper coins ..	9,53,002
Two pie ,, ,,	2,59,88,200
One pie ,, ,, ..	2

Gold coins are now used only for presentation purposes. And there is in the State no paper money. Salaries and wages are paid in O. S. rupees, and the consequences of this sort of payment are sometimes amusing. For instance, I was calling one day at a house where a government servant resided, and I was surprised to see him stagger into the room with a large bag in each hand. Asked what made him bend and sway, he replied "My salary", and he poured on to the carpet a load of O. S. rupees that would eventually go to the local branch of the Bank of Bengal and be placed there to his credit.

The official rate of exchange between the Hyderabad rupee and the British Government rupee varies to-day between 16 and 20; and the official standard in 1,000 O. S. rupees is 818·1 pure silver and the rest alloy.

Into the intricacies of the copper coinage I will not enter, for the *ghandas* and *dubs* that are the delight of servants, I found to be in the districts a great nuisance. Thus if a railway ticket was a little more than a rupee, I received from 80 to 90 small copper coins, and the servant and the ticket babu then began to quarrel over the rate of exchange and the number of *dubs* that I ought to have. Only in Hyderabad City and Secunderabad can a railway ticket be taken in British Government money, and at the small stations it is difficult and sometimes impossible to change B. G. rupees into O. S. rupees. As to a B. G. ten-rupee note, they look at it with suspicion in the districts, and the sowcars there say:—" I have no use for it."

The Stamp Department.

This Department is under the care of the Mint Master, and in it postage stamps, stamped envelopes and postcards, summons, receipt and *hundi* stamps and stamp paper are made. The Government made by this department during 1321 Fasli (1911-1912 A.D.) a profit of Rs. 8,17,221. There is an Inspector-General of Registration and Stamps, and the Government surplus from the Registration Department in 1321 Fasli (1911-1912 A.D.), was Rs. 43,595.

Weights and Measures Department.

This Department has only recently come into existence, and the primary standards and the necessary fine balances and appliances for the accurate manufacture and checking of weights and measures have not yet arrived from London. The work undertaken in this department will be the manufacture of standard weights for checking the weights and measures used throughout the Dominions, and the manufacture of weights and measures for use by the public.

THE ELECTRICITY DEPARTMENT.

This Department, which is still in its infancy, owes its inception to Mr. R. Loraine Gamlen, the energetic Mint Master. He found that the power of the engines provided by Sir George Casson Walker for the purposes of minting was in excess of the requirements, and he obtained from His Highness's government sanction to start an electric supply for the neighbourhood, using the surplus power available in the Mint for driving the electric machinery. First, the King Koti Palace and the Residency were lighted by electricity; and then, when the Viceroy visited Hyderabad in September 1913, the Falaknama Palace, the Bund and the City were lighted in the same way. More machinery has been bought, and, at the present time, the Mint Master is in England, perfecting the arrangements of the Electricity Department.

CHAPTER XVIII.

MISCELLANEOUS.

Mahomedan and English Rule.

NEEDLESS to say, the things that interested me most, while travelling in the districts, were the differences that I noticed there between Mahomedan and English rule. I came to the conclusion that the former is the most popular with Hindus, and chiefly so because it interferes the least with their customs and habits. In British India, Hindus are always being hustled by energetic young English civilians and "chartered hands," who want to have everything done in a hurry and done according to their own customs. But in His Highness's Dominions, Hindus are not interfered with, unless they do something very flagrant.

Now I feel sure that in British India the Irregular Forces, which are of little use and which cost His Highness's government annually 23½ lakhs of rupees, would long ago have been abolished, and that the jagirdars would, many years before this, have been shorn of such privileges as their own Law Courts and prisons. The small jagirdars are, it seems to me, the white elephant of the Hyderabad State at the present time, for they retard general progress and, in most cases, take no interest in the education of their ryots.

And I am not at all sure that an excessive regard for privileges conferred in by-gone ages is good for the masses. In fact I noticed in the districts an inertia that I have not found anywhere in British India. In vain I looked for modern Hindu temples. The ruins of old ones I found, but I saw few, if any, Hindu temples that have been built during the time of the Nizams. Even in religion the Hindus appear to be apathetic under Mahomedan rule. Mosques I saw everywhere, but when I asked :—" Where do the Hindus worship ? " I was shewn ruined temples on hills outside cities, or I was told :—" The Hindus go to the Godavari—their sacred river—to say their prayers."

Perhaps it is good for the Hindus to be hustled. I do not know. Bombs are unpleasant. I cannot imagine a Nizam riding alone to meet a Wat Tyler, like Richard the Second of England; yet without such people as Wat Tyler where would England be now?

THE PURDAH SYSTEM.

English people are wont to say that the purdah system is at the root of all backwardness in India, and that, "the hope of India lies in educating its women." I do not care to argue this point, more especially in the case of the Hyderabad State, where all women—both Mahomedans and Hindus—of the higher classes (with a few notable exceptions), live behind the curtain. We have seen in the new census that Hindu working-women in the Dominions are engaged in almost every kind of business, and that they show a marked aptitude for trade and possess a keen money-making instinct. And we have read in the education reports that the schools for girls of the upper classes in Hyderabad city are as good, if not better, than similar places in British India. No doubt, there is in the districts a very strong prejudice against female education; and the census suggests that one reason for this is the jealousy of Hindu and Mahomedan men. "If a woman can write a letter, then she may write a love-letter," says the census.

One would like to hear what such people as "Taj," the gifted authoress of "Zorah," and Mrs. Sarojini Naidu, the well-known Hindu poetess of Hyderabad, think on these subjects. At any rate, there is in the Hyderabad State no great army of prostitutes, such as one finds all over Europe.

The Missionaries.

There are many missionaries in the Hyderabad State, more, I think, than can be found in any similar area in British India. The greater number of them come from America, and are in consequence, pushing and energetic people. That missionaries are doing good work in raising the lowest classes in the social scale throughout His Highness's Dominions there can be no doubt, and more especially by their hospitals do they reach the hearts of the so-called "outcasts" and gain a lasting influence. There is in the Hyderabad State no Missionary Year Book, and Methodists, Baptists and Wesleyans seem to know little about anything further than their own particular mission. So I will briefly describe the largest mission in the State, namely, the Wesleyan Methodist Evangelistic Mission at Medak. This mission began its work in 1887, when Medak was fifty miles from any railway station, and its remarkable success is due to the three pioneer workers, the Rev. Charles Posnett, his sister, Miss Posnett, and her friend, Miss Sara Harris. When Mr. Posnett in 1887 applied for a piece of land at Medak on which to build "an outcast church," the government of that period gave him the city dunghill! Now he is a person whom the government of to-day fully appreciates. And even among the people whom he desired to help, Mr. Posnett met with much opposition until the doctor, Miss Posnett, and the hospital nurse, Miss Sara Harris, had won the confidence of the women of Medak by their medical and surgical treatment. In 1903 a large Zenana Hospital was built, chiefly with the help of Mr. Posnett's relations and friends in England, and last year (1913), 831 in-patients and 13,800 out-patients were treated in this hospital and 2,660 in the village dispensaries round Medak. There are now in the boarding schools of the Mission 113 boys and 125 girls, and in the 51 village schools 701 children, and in the Theological College, 41 students. A great deal of famine relief work has been done by this mission, and most of the large buildings in the mission compound were built during famines.

Among Mahomedans the missionaries do not work, but among the lowest classes of Hindus they make in the Hyderabad State a yearly increasing number of converts.

And it is not generally known that the Indian Protestant bishop, who, two years ago, was consecrated with so much pomp in St. Paul's Cathedral, Calcutta, lives in His Highness's Dominions. Most people think that Bishop Azariah resides in British India, but as a matter of fact he is at Dornakal, in the Hyderabad State.

An impatient and zealous young American missionary made not long ago some foolish remarks on His Highness's government because he could not obtain, in hot haste, a piece of land on which to build a church. So it may be well to state that all religions are treated alike in the Hyderabad State, that churches, as well as mosques and temples, there receive donations, and that the delay in granting permission to erect a religious edifice has its root in the fact that His Highness's government makes no religious favourites.

The Nizamiah Observatory.

This observatory began with two large telescopes and other instruments which were presented to His Highness the late Nizam by the late Nawab Zaffer Jung Bahadur; and owes its development to Mr. A. B. Chatwood, B.SC., F.R.A.S., A.M.I.C.E., who was appointed State astronomer in 1908. Having built, organised, and equipped an observatory, Mr. Chatwood undertook, with the consent of His Highness's government, a portion of the vast piece of astronomical work that is known as the *Carte Photographique du Ciel*, or the "Astrographic Chart;" and with this work he is busy at the present time.

The Astrographic Chart consists of a catalogue of all stars to the eleventh magnitude—about ten millions—and a map of 22,054 sheets showing, also, very much smaller stars, two hundred millions in all, perhaps.

The Post Office.

The Hyderabad State has its own postal service and issues stamps, and the government has managed this department since 1869, when important reforms were introduced into it by Sir Salar Jung I.

In 1321 Fasli (1911-1912 A.D.), the number of postal articles carried totalled 13,333,618, the mileage over which mails were carried by rail was during that time 1,195 and the mileage by road was 4,976.

There is a British Post Office in Hyderabad city (Chadarghat), and small British Government Post Offices are scattered throughout the State, and letters bearing English postage stamps are conveyed free from the State Post Offices to the nearest British Post Office or railway mail service section.

THE RAILWAYS.

The Great Indian Peninsula Railway in the south and west, and the Madras and East Coast Railways in the south and east, are united by the Nizam's Guaranteed State Railway, which runs from Wadi in the west to Bezwāda in the east. This railway is owned and worked by a company under a guarantee from the Hyderabad State, and the same company works the metre-gauge line which connects the capital with Manmad, in the Nasik district of Bombay. There are also branch lines from Husain Saugar to Hyderabad, Dornakal to Singareni, and Purna

Junction to Hingoli ; and a line is now being constructed from the capital to Gadag, *viâ* Mahbubnagar and Raichur. In the Barsi Light Railway the government has no financial interest.

During 1320-1321 Fasli (1910-1912 A.D.), the whole of the interest guaranteed by government was reimbursed by the company, and the government also received £25,440 as their share of the surplus profits towards the liquidation of the Contingent Liability Account. The total sum outstanding against the company in the Contingent Liability Account at the end of 1912 was £2,102,961 including simple interest at five per cent.

Having travelled much on the State Railway, I may say that it is slow but safe, and one need never be afraid of experiencing a railway accident on it. People do not travel as much in the Nizam's Dominions as they do in British India, consequently one can sleep at night. But electric fans there are none, and water runs short during hot weather, and rules concerning the conveyance of luggage in the van do not exist. Thus, on one occasion I saw the " traps " of a missionary Sahib removed from a first-class carriage, and they consisted of two steel trunks, one portmanteau, two tins of kerosene, four lamps, a small bundle of sticks and umbrellas, a large bundle of bedding, a zinc bath filled with kitchen utensils, a tennis racket, two hats, and a tiffin basket.

In the Districts.

In conclusion, I would like to say how much interested I was in all that I saw in the districts. There one can learn more in six weeks than during six months spent in the capital; and chiefly so, I think, because government officials in the districts are much less reticent than is the case in Hyderabad city and its suburbs. Having read of the bribery and corruption that existed among talukdars and tahsildars in the time of Sir Salar Jung I, I was not prepared to find these gentlemen so up-to-date and so efficient. The Subedars of the four divisions I did not see, because I visited Warangal, Medak, Gulbarga and Aurangabad during the cold weather, and they were all on tour. But among talukdars and tahsildars I moved freely, and although I had no introductions, I was made welcome and shewn everything.

And this is what I noticed. Everywhere the machinery of administration is excellent, but so far the people in the districts cannot live up to it. They lag, and when I asked the reason for this sluggishness, I was generally told that the small jagirdars and the fat sowcars are at the root of the slow progress that is being made at present. Things familiar to me in British India I found everywhere, but not so highly developed as they are under English rule.

And I may add that some of the ancient customs in the capital were sharply criticised by the Mahomedan talukdars and tahsildars; in fact, the Mahomedan gentlemen who administer the districts appear to be in advance of much that now goes on in the capital, and if His Highness the Nizam desires to quicken the speed of the State coach, and remove some of its ancient fittings, I am sure that he will find support among the up-to-date government officials in the districts. And with these hopeful remarks I will close this little book, adding all good wishes for His Highness's government, which has, no doubt, the true interests of the people in the Dominions at heart, and wishing for H. H. the Nizam a long and prosperous reign, during which he may see the Hyderabad State prosper and develop.

INDIAN SNAPSHOTS.

THIRD EDITION.

"A most fair, impartial and most interesting book."—*The Daily News.*

"The author of this book has not, like some others, been led about by Congress-Baboos, seditious editors, disaffected lawyers or discontented students. It would take pages to refer to the sound and sane things said, and the excellent judgment given in this little volume. In short, this is one of the best books on India published for some time."—*The Pall Mall Gazette.*

"There is much that may be studied from this book, especially by Englishman, to whom indeed, it reveals 'Hidden India in a fair and faithful manner.'"—*The Indian Patriot.*

"This little volume by Mr. Law gives us in an easy, simple style, many a valuable insight into the character of the natives of India and also into the barriers which separate the sympathies of the Indians and of their British rulers. Mr. Law did not merely wander idly through the regular tourist tracts, but lived among the people of whom he writes, visited them in their homes and made many friendships among them. He was able to appreciate their aspirations, and he seeks above all to give the readers of his book a picture of the position from the view of the subject races."—*The Age.*

"Looking as he did beneath the surface, it is no wonder that Mr. John Law's impressions of India should be of a more abiding interest and differ considerably from those of the ordinary Englishman. He is free from all affectation and employs a crisp diction to write what he feels. The result is a singularly lively volume."—*The Parsi.*

THE HOROSCOPE.

In this book it is shown how the horoscopes of two brothers, Banda and Tikri Delgama, who were descended from the royal line of Kandy, worked out. The author gives us an admirable account of Ceylon, its people, its physical beauties, and its religion. Clearly he has studied the Buddhist faith deeply, and in "the little monk" (Tikri) he has created a most lovable character, setting forth that religion in a most attractive light. The end of the two brothers, who died together, is most affecting. Banda has been bitten by a mad dog, and is going distraught. The younger brother, regardless of self, tends him to the last, and then, worn out with his exertions, expires, fully sustained by the faith that was in him. The little monk cried in his soul, "I come," "I give myself up," "I trust."—*The Literary World.*

The scene of this novel is entirely laid in Ceylon. Ceylon stories, with which it might be compared, are few, if any exist. There is plenty of local colouring: the writer shows a knowledge of at least some portion of the colony's history, of its chief products, of the manner of life, and, above all, of the dominant Buddhism and its practical operation. So far we might have been describing a Gazetteer. But the book is a story full of human developments. A Sinhalese gentleman, descended from the deposed Kandyan dynasty, proprietor of an encumbered estate, loses his wife, is left with two little boys, and devotes himself to their welfare. The story turns on the evolution of the horoscope of the elder son: a superstitious regard attaches to horoscopes in Eastern countries. This elder boy is, contrary to an English planter's advice, sent to a Christian College, and eventually, after his father's death, becomes a Christian. The younger becomes a Buddhist monk. Their mutual devotion is touching. Their characters and careers are well drawn. The life of the elder is hardly a success: the moral is that he would have done better by adhering to Sinhalese ways. His Sinhalese wife is amusing in her ambitious. The younger brother is the stronger character. His trust in his faith is unshaken: his attachment to his stricken brother is most pathetic. The interest is well sustained to the end. The Buddhism is prominent, but not overdone. How many understand what Nirvâna means ? It is " taught that Desire leads men to be born again and again, and that by killing Desire a man can escape from re-births and enter Nirvâna"—the deathless state.—*The Academy.*